DOVER · THRIFT · EDITIONS

Early Poems

WILLIAM BUTLER YEATS

DOVER PUBLICATIONS, INC.
New York

DOVER THRIFT EDITIONS

GENERAL EDITOR: STANLEY APPELBAUM
EDITOR OF THIS VOLUME: SHANE WELLER

Bibliographical Note

This Dover edition, first published in 1993, contains all the lyric poems from the following W. B. Yeats volumes: *The Wind Among the Reeds* (second edition), Elkin Mathews, London, 1899; *In the Seven Woods: Being Poems Chiefly of the Irish Heroic Age*, The Dun Emer Press, Dundrum, 1903; *The Green Helmet and Other Poems*, The Cuala Press, Churchtown, Dundrum, 1910; *Poems*, T. Fisher Unwin, London, 1912; and *Responsibilities: Poems and a Play*, The Cuala Press, Churchtown, Dundrum, 1914.

The Note, the footnotes and the alphabetical lists of titles and first lines were prepared specially for the present edition.

Library of Congress Cataloging-in-Publication Data

Yeats, W. B. (William Butler), 1865–1939.
  Early poems / William Butler Yeats.
      p.   cm. — (Dover thrift editions)
  ISBN 0-486-27808-5 (pbk.)
  I. Title.   II. Series.
PR5902.A3   1993
821'.8—dc20   93-21798
                                                         CIP

Manufactured in the United States of America
Dover Publications, Inc., 31 East 2nd Street, Mineola, N.Y. 11501

Note

THE NOBEL LAUREATE William Butler Yeats (1865–1939) is perhaps the greatest modern English-language poet, whose verse demonstrates both technical virtuosity and an extraordinary range (from love songs and ballads to meditations on time, history and the spiritual). Besides the lyric and narrative poems, he also wrote plays, essays, stories, autobiographies and philosophy. For his subject matter and vocabulary he drew heavily on Irish mythology, contemporary Irish history and mystical philosophy.

The present edition contains all the lyric poetry from Yeats's first six collections of verse: *Crossways* (1889), *The Rose* (1893),* *The Wind Among the Reeds* (1899), *In the Seven Woods* (1903), *The Green Helmet and Other Poems* (1910) and *Responsibilities* (1914). Yeats devoted considerable energy throughout his career to revising poems; thus, the versions and the poem titles found here sometimes differ quite markedly from both earlier and later ones. (The editions reprinted are identified on the copyright page.) In addition, a few poems included under the above headings in *The Collected Poems* (1933) do not appear here in any form.

---

* *Crossways* and *The Rose* were not published as individual volumes; these titles were established by Yeats in the volume *Poems* (1895).

Contents

The Wind Among the Reeds (1899)

In the Seven Woods (1903)

The Green Helmet and Other Poems (1910)

Responsibilities (1914)

CROSSWAYS

"The stars are threshed, and the souls are threshed from their husks."
WILLIAM BLAKE.

To A. E.

The Song of the Happy Shepherd

The woods of Arcady are dead,
And over is their antique joy;
Of old the world on dreaming fed;
Gray Truth is now her painted toy;
Yet still she turns her restless head:
But O, sick children of the world,
Of all the many changing things
In dreary dancing past us whirled,
To the cracked tune that Chronos sings,
Words alone are certain good.
Where are now the warring kings,
Word be-mockers?—By the Rood
Where are now the warring kings?
An idle word is now their glory,
By the stammering schoolboy said,
Reading some entangled story:
The kings of the old time are fled.
The wandering earth herself may be
Only a sudden flaming word,
In clanging space a moment heard,
Troubling the endless reverie.

Then nowise worship dusty deeds,
Nor seek; for this is also sooth;
To hunger fiercely after truth,
Lest all thy toiling only breeds
New dreams, new dreams; there is no truth
Saving in thine own heart. Seek, then,
No learning from the starry men,

1

Who follow with the optic glass
The whirling ways of stars that pass—
Seek, then, for this is also sooth,
No word of theirs—the cold star-bane
Has cloven and rent their hearts in twain,
And dead is all their human truth.
Go gather by the humming-sea
Some twisted, echo-harbouring shell,
And to its lips thy story tell,
And they thy comforters will be,
Rewarding in melodious guile,
Thy fretful words a little while,
Till they shall singing fade in ruth,
And die a pearly brotherhood;
For words alone are certain good:
Sing, then, for this is also sooth.

I must be gone: there is a grave
Where daffodil and lily wave,
And I would please the hapless faun,
Buried under the sleepy ground,
With mirthful songs before the dawn.
His shouting days with mirth were crowned;
And still I dream he treads the lawn,
Walking ghostly in the dew,
Pierced by my glad singing through,
My songs of old earth's dreamy youth:
But ah! she dreams not now; dream thou!
For fair are poppies on the brow:
Dream, dream, for this is also sooth.

The Sad Shepherd

There was a man whom Sorrow named his friend,
And he, of his high comrade Sorrow dreaming,
Went walking with slow steps along the gleaming
And humming sands, where windy surges wend:
And he called loudly to the stars to bend
From their pale thrones and comfort him, but they

Among themselves laugh on and sing alway:
And then the man whom Sorrow named his friend
Cried out, *Dim sea, hear my most piteous story!*
The sea swept on and cried her old cry still,
Rolling along in dreams from hill to hill;
He fled the persecution of her glory
And, in a far-off, gentle valley stopping,
Cried all his story to the dewdrops glistening,
But naught they heard, for they are always listening,
The dewdrops, for the sound of their own dropping.
And then the man whom Sorrow named his friend,
Sought once again the shore, and found a shell,
And thought, *I will my heavy story tell*
Till my own words, re-echoing, shall send
Their sadness through a hollow, pearly heart;
And my own tale again for me shall sing,
And my own whispering words be comforting,
And lo! my ancient burden may depart.
Then he sang softly nigh the pearly rim;
But the sad dweller by the sea-ways lone
Changed all he sang to inarticulate moan
Among her wildering whirls, forgetting him.

The Cloak, the Boat, and the Shoes

"What do you make so fair and bright?"

"I make the cloak of Sorrow:
"O, lovely to see in all men's sight
"Shall be the cloak of Sorrow,
"In all men's sight."

"What do you build with sails for flight?"

"I build a boat for Sorrow,
"O, swift on the seas all day and night
"Saileth the rover Sorrow,
"All day and night."

"What do you weave with wool so white?"

"I weave the shoes of Sorrow,
"Soundless shall be the footfall light
"In all men's ears of Sorrow,
"Sudden and light."

Anashuya and Vijaya

A little Indian temple in the Golden Age. Around it a garden; around that the forest. ANASHUYA, *the young priestess, kneeling within the temple.*

ANASHUYA

Send peace on all the lands and flickering corn.—
O, may tranquillity walk by his elbow
When wandering in the forest, if he love
No other.—Hear, and may the indolent flocks
Be plentiful.—And if he love another,
May panthers end him.—Hear, and load our king
With wisdom hour by hour.—May we two stand,
When we are dead, beyond the setting suns,
A little from the other shades apart,
With mingling hair, and play upon one lute.

VIJAYA [*entering and throwing a lily at her*]

Hail! hail, my Anashuya.

ANASHUYA

            No: be still.
I, priestess of this temple, offer up
Prayers for the land.

VIJAYA

            I will wait here, Amrita.

ANASHUYA

By mighty Brahma's ever rustling robe,
Who is Amrita? Sorrow of all sorrows!
Another fills your mind.

VIJAYA

            My mother's name.

ANASHUYA [*sings, coming out of the temple*]

A sad, sad thought went by me slowly:
Sigh, O you little stars! O, sigh and shake your blue apparel!
The sad, sad thought has gone from me now wholly:
Sing, O you little stars! O, sing and raise your rapturous carol
To mighty Brahma, he who made you many as the sands,
And laid you on the gates of evening with his quiet hands.

[*Sits down on the steps of the temple.*]

Vijaya, I have brought my evening rice;
The sun has laid his chin on the gray wood,
Weary, with all his poppies gathered round him.

VIJAYA

The hour when Kama,[1] full of sleepy laughter,
Rises, and showers abroad his fragrant arrows,
Piercing the twilight with their murmuring barbs.

ANASHUYA

See how the sacred old flamingoes come,
Painting with shadow all the marble steps:
Aged and wise, they seek their wonted perches
Within the temple, devious walking, made
To wander by their melancholy minds.
Yon tall one eyes my supper; swiftly chase him
Far, far away. I named him after you.
He is a famous fisher; hour by hour
He ruffles with his bill the minnowed streams.
Ah! there he snaps my rice. I told you so.
Now cuff him off. He's off! A kiss for you,
Because you saved my rice. Have you no thanks?

VIJAYA [*sings*]

Sing you of her, O first few stars,
Whom Brahma, touching with his finger, praises, for you hold
The van of wandering quiet; ere you be too calm and old,
Sing, turning in your cars,

---

[1] The Hindu god of love.

Sing, till you raise your hands and sigh, and from your car heads
    peer,
With all your whirling hair, and drop many an azure tear.

ANASHUYA

What know the pilots of the stars of tears?

VIJAYA

Their faces are all worn, and in their eyes
Flashes the fire of sadness, for they see
The icicles that famish all the north,
Where men lie frozen in the glimmering snow;
And in the flaming forests cower the lion
And lioness, with all their whimpering cubs;
And, ever pacing on the verge of things,
The phantom, Beauty, in a mist of tears;
While we alone have round us woven woods,
And feel the softness of each other's hand,
Amrita, while——

ANASHUYA [*going away from him*]

               Ah me, you love another,

                       [*Bursting into tears.*]

And may some dreadful ill befall her quick!

VIJAYA

I loved another; now I love no other.
Among the mouldering of ancient woods
You live, and on the village border she,
With her old father the blind wood-cutter;
I saw her standing in her door but now.

ANASHUYA

Vijaya, swear to love her never more.

VIJAYA

Ay, ay.

ANASHUYA

      Swear by the parents of the gods,
Dread oath, who dwell on sacred Himalay,

On the far Golden Peak; enormous shapes,
Who still were old when the great sea was young;
On their vast faces mystery and dreams;
Their hair along the mountains rolled and filled
From year to year by the unnumbered nests
Of aweless birds, and round their stirless feet
The joyous flocks of deer and antelope,
Who never hear the unforgiving hound.
Swear!

VIJAYA

      By the parents of the gods, I swear.

ANASHUYA [*sings*]

I have forgiven, O new star!
Maybe you have not heard of us, you have come forth so newly,
You hunter of the fields afar!
Ah, you will know my loved one by his hunter's arrows truly,
Shoot on him shafts of quietness, that he may ever keep
An inner laughter, and may kiss his hands to me in sleep.

Farewell, Vijaya. Nay, no word, no word;
I, priestess of this temple, offer up
Prayers for the land.

                        [VIJAYA *goes.*]

            O Brahma, guard in sleep
The merry lambs and the complacent kine,
The flies below the leaves, and the young mice
In the tree roots, and all the sacred flocks
Of red flamingo; and my love, Vijaya;
And may no restless fay with fidget finger
Trouble his sleeping: give him dreams of me.

The Indian upon God

I passed along the water's edge below the humid trees,
My spirit rocked in evening light, the rushes round my knees,
My spirit rocked in sleep and sighs; and saw the moorfowl pace

All dripping on a grassy slope, and saw them cease to chase
Each other round in circles, and heard the eldest speak:
Who holds the world between His bill and made us strong or weak
Is an undying moorfowl, and He lives beyond the sky.
The rains are from His dripping wing, the moonbeams from His eye.
I passed a little further on and heard a lotus talk:
Who made the world and ruleth it, He hangeth on a stalk,
For I am in His image made, and all this tinkling tide
Is but a sliding drop of rain between His petals wide.
A little way within the gloom a roebuck raised his eyes
Brimful of starlight, and he said: *The Stamper of the Skies,*
He is a gentle roebuck; for how else, I pray, could He
Conceive a thing so sad and soft, a gentle thing like me?
I passed a little further on and heard a peacock say:
Who made the grass and made the worms and made my feathers gay,
He is a monstrous peacock, and He waveth all the night
His languid tail above us, lit with myriad spots of light.

The Indian to His Love

The island dreams under the dawn
And great boughs drop tranquillity;
The peahens dance on a smooth lawn,
A parrot sways upon a tree,
Raging at his own image in the enamelled sea.

Here we will moor our lonely ship
And wander ever with woven hands,
Murmuring softly lip to lip,
Along the grass, along the sands,
Murmuring how far away are the unquiet lands:

How we alone of mortals are
Hid under quiet bows apart,
While our love grows an Indian star,
A meteor of the burning heart,
One with the tide that gleams, the wings that gleam and dart,

The heavy boughs, the burnished dove
That moans and sighs a hundred days:

How when we die our shades will rove,
When eve has hushed the feathered ways,
With vapoury footsole among the water's drowsy blaze.

The Falling of the Leaves

Autumn is over the long leaves that love us,
And over the mice in the barley sheaves;
Yellow the leaves of the rowan above us,
And yellow the wet wild-strawberry leaves.

The hour of the waning of love has beset us,
And weary and worn are our sad souls now;
Let us part, ere the season of passion forget us,
With a kiss and a tear on thy drooping brow.

Ephemera

"Your eyes that once were never weary of mine
"Are bowed in sorrow under pendulous lids,
"Because our love is waning."

And then she:
"Although our love is waning, let us stand
"By the lone border of the lake once more,
"Together in that hour of gentleness
"When the poor tired child, Passion, falls asleep:
"How far away the stars seem, and how far
"Is our first kiss, and ah, how old my heart!"

Pensive they paced along the faded leaves,
While slowly he whose hand held hers replied:
"Passion has often worn our wandering hearts."

The woods were round them, and the yellow leaves
Fell like faint meteors in the gloom, and once
A rabbit old and lame limped down the path;
Autumn was over him: and now they stood
On the lone border of the lake once more:

Turning, he saw that she had thrust dead leaves
Gathered in silence, dewy as her eyes,
In bosom and hair.

                    "Ah, do not mourn," he said,
"That we are tired, for other loves await us;
"Hate on and love through unrepining hours.
"Before us lies eternity; our souls
"Are love, and a continual farewell."

The Madness of King Goll

I sat on cushioned otter skin:
My word was law from Ith to Emen,
And shook at Invar Amargin
The hearts of the world-troubling seamen,
And drove tumult and war away
From girl and boy and man and beast;
The fields grew fatter day by day,
The wild fowl of the air increased;
And every ancient Ollave[1] said,
While he bent down his fading head,
"He drives away the Northern cold."
*They will not hush, the leaves a-flutter round me, the beech leaves
        old.*

I sat and mused and drank sweet wine;
A herdsman came from inland valleys,
Crying, the pirates drove his swine
To fill their dark-beaked hollow galleys.
I called my battle-breaking men,
And my loud brazen battle-cars
From rolling vale and rivery glen;
And under the blinking of the stars
Fell on the pirates by the deep,
And hurled them in the gulph of sleep:
These hands won many a torque of gold.
*They will not hush, the leaves a-flutter round me, the beech leaves
        old.*

---

[1] Irish poet.

But slowly, as I shouting slew
And trampled in the bubbling mire,
In my most secret spirit grew
A whirling and a wandering fire:
I stood: keen stars above me shone,
Around me shone keen eyes of men:
I laughed aloud and hurried on
By rocky shore and rushy fen;
I laughed because birds fluttered by,
And starlight gleamed, and clouds flew high,
And rushes waved and waters rolled.
*They will not hush, the leaves a-flutter round me, the beech leaves
    old.*

And now I wander in the woods
When summer gluts the golden bees,
Or in autumnal solitudes
Arise the leopard-coloured trees;
Or when along the wintry strands
The cormorants shiver on their rocks;
I wander on, and wave my hands,
And sing, and shake my heavy locks.
The gray wolf knows me; by one ear
I lead along the woodland deer;
The hares run by me growing bold.
*They will not hush, the leaves a-flutter round me, the beech leaves
    old.*

I came upon a little town,
That slumbered in the harvest moon,
And passed a-tiptoe up and down,
Murmuring, to a fitful tune,
How I have followed, night and day,
A tramping of tremendous feet,
And saw where this old tympan lay,
Deserted on a doorway seat,
And bore it to the woods with me;
Of some unhuman misery
Our married voices wildly trolled.
*They will not hush, the leaves a-flutter round me, the beech leaves
    old.*

I sang how, when day's toil is done,
Orchil[1] shakes out her long dark hair
That hides away the dying sun
And sheds faint odours through the air:
When my hand passed from wire to wire
It quenched, with sound like falling dew,
The whirling and the wandering fire;
But lift a mournful ulalu,
For the kind wires are torn and still,
And I must wander wood and hill
Through summer's heat and winter's cold.
*They will not hush, the leaves a-flutter round me, the beech leaves
    old.*

The Stolen Child

Where dips the rocky highland
Of Sleuth Wood in the lake,
There lies a leafy island
Where flapping herons wake
The drowsy water rats;
There we've hid our faery vats,
Full of berries,
And of reddest stolen cherries.
Come away, O human child!
To the waters and the wild
With a faery, hand in hand,
For the world's more full of weeping than you can understand.

Where the wave of moonlight glosses
The dim gray sands with light,
Far off by furthest Rosses
We foot it all the night,
Weaving olden dances,
Mingling hands and mingling glances
Till the moon has taken flight;
To and fro we leap
And chase the frothy bubbles,

---

[1] A sorceress.

While the world is full of troubles
And is anxious in its sleep.
Come away, O human child!
To the waters and the wild
With a faery, hand in hand,
For the world's more full of weeping than you can understand.

Where the wandering water gushes
From the hills above Glen-Car,
In pools among the rushes
That scarce could bathe a star,
We seek for slumbering trout
And whispering in their ears
Give them unquiet dreams;
Leaning softly out
From ferns that drop their tears
Over the young streams.
Come away, O human child!
To the waters and the wild
With a faery, hand in hand,
For the world's more full of weeping than you can understand.

Away with us he's going,
The solemn-eyed:
He'll hear no more the lowing
Of the calves on the warm hillside;
Or the kettle on the hob
Sing peace into his breast,
Or see the brown mice bob
Round and round the oatmeal-chest.
For he comes, the human child,
To the waters and the wild
With a faery, hand in hand,
From a world more full of weeping than he can understand.

To an Isle in the Water

Shy one, shy one,
Shy one of my heart,
She moves in the firelight
Pensively apart.

She carries in the dishes,
And lays them in a row.
To an isle in the water
With her would I go.

She carries in the candles,
And lights the curtained room,
Shy in the doorway
And shy in the gloom;

And shy as a rabbit,
Helpful and shy.
To an isle in the water
With her would I fly.

Down by the Salley Gardens

Down by the salley[1] gardens my love and I did meet;
She passed the salley gardens with little snow-white feet.
She bid me take love easy, as the leaves grow on the tree;
But I, being young and foolish, with her would not agree.

In a field by the river my love and I did stand,
And on my leaning shoulder she laid her snow-white hand.
She bid me take life easy, as the grass grows on the weirs;
But I was young and foolish, and now am full of tears.

The Meditation of the Old Fisherman

You waves, though you dance by my feet like children at play,
Though you glow and you glance, though you purr and you dart;
In the Junes that were warmer than these are, the waves were more
    gay,
When I was a boy with never a crack in my heart.

The herring are not in the tides as they were of old;
My sorrow! for many a creak gave the creel[2] in the cart

---

[1] Willow.
[2] Fish basket.

That carried the take to Sligo town to be sold,
When I was a boy with never a crack in my heart.

And ah, you proud maiden, you are not so fair when his oar
Is heard on the water, as they were, the proud and apart,
Who paced in the eve by the nets on the pebbly shore,
When I was a boy with never a crack in my heart.

The Ballad of Father O'Hart

Good Father John O'Hart
In penal days rode out
To a shoneen[1] who had free lands
And his own snipe and trout.

In trust took he John's lands;
Sleiveens[2] were all his race;
And he gave them as dowers to his daughters,
And they married beyond their place.

But Father John went up,
And Father John went down;
And he wore small holes in his shoes,
And he wore large holes in his gown.

All loved him, only the shoneen,
Whom the devils have by the hair,
From the wives, and the cats, and the children,
To the birds in the white of the air.

The birds, for he opened their cages
As he went up and down;
And he said with a smile, "Have peace now";
And he went his way with a frown.

But if when any one died
Came keeners[3] hoarser than rooks,
He bade them give over their keening;
For he was a man of books.

---

[1] Upstart. [Yeats]
[2] Mean fellows. [Yeats]
[3] Hired mourners.

And these were the works of John,
When weeping score by score,
People came into Coloony;
For he'd died at ninety-four.

There was no human keening;
The birds from Knocknarea
And the world round Knocknashee
Came keening in that day.

The young birds and old birds
Came flying, heavy and sad;
Keening in from Tiraragh,
Keening from Ballinafad;

Keening from Inishmurray,
Nor stayed for bite or sup;
This way were all reproved
Who dig old customs up.

The Ballad of Moll Magee

Come round me, little childer;
There, don't fling stones at me
Because I mutter as I go;
But pity Moll Magee.

My man was a poor fisher
With shore lines in the say;[1]
My work was saltin' herrings
The whole of the long day.

And sometimes from the saltin' shed,
I scarce could drag my feet
Under the blessed moonlight,
Along the pebbly street.

I'd always been but weakly,
And my baby was just born;
A neighbour minded her by day,
I minded her till morn.

---

[1] Sea.

I lay upon my baby;
Ye little childer dear,
I looked on my cold baby
When the morn grew frosty and clear.

A weary woman sleeps so hard!
My man grew red and pale,
And gave me money, and bade me go
To my own place, Kinsale.

He drove me out and shut the door,
And gave his curse to me;
I went away in silence,
No neighbour could I see.

The windows and the doors were shut,
One star shone faint and green;
The little straws were turnin' round
Across the bare boreen. [1]

I went away in silence:
Beyond old Martin's byre
I saw a kindly neighbour
Blowin' her mornin' fire.

She drew from me my story—
My money's all used up,
And still, with pityin', scornin' eye,
She gives me bite and sup.

She says my man will surely come,
And fetch me home agin;
But always, as I'm movin' round,
Without doors or within,

Pilin' the wood or pilin' the turf,
Or goin' to the well,
I'm thinkin' of my baby
And keenin' to mysel'.

And sometimes I am sure she knows
When, openin' wide His door,

---

[1] Lane.

God lights the stars, His candles,
And looks upon the poor.

So now, ye little childer,
Ye won't fling stones at me;
But gather with your shinin' looks
And pity Moll Magee.

The Ballad of the Foxhunter

"Now lay me in a cushioned chair
"And carry me, you four,
"With cushions here and cushions there,
"To see the world once more.

"And some one from the stables bring
"My Dermot dear and brown,
"And lead him gently in a ring,
"And gently up and down.

"Now leave the chair upon the grass:
"Bring hound and huntsman here,
"And I on this strange road will pass,
"Filled full of ancient cheer."

His eyelids droop, his head falls low,
His old eyes cloud with dreams;
The sun upon all things that grow
Pours round in sleepy streams.

Brown Dermot treads upon the lawn,
And to the armchair goes,
And now the old man's dreams are gone,
He smooths the long brown nose.

And now moves many a pleasant tongue
Upon his wasted hands,
For leading aged hounds and young
The huntsman near him stands.

"My huntsman, Rody, blow the horn,
"And make the hills reply."
The huntsman loosens on the morn
A gay and wandering cry.

A fire is in the old man's eyes,
His fingers move and sway,
And when the wandering music dies
They hear him feebly say,

"My huntsman, Rody, blow the horn,
"And make the hills reply."
"I cannot blow upon my horn,
"I can but weep and sigh."

The servants round his cushioned place
Are with new sorrow wrung;
And hounds are gazing on his face,
Both aged hounds and young.

One blind hound only lies apart
On the sun-smitten grass;
He holds deep commune with his heart:
The moments pass and pass;

The blind hound with a mournful din
Lifts slow his wintry head;
The servants bear the body in;
The hounds wail for the dead.

THE ROSE

"Sero te amavi, Pulchritudo tam antiqua et tam nova! Sero te amavi."[1]

S. AUGUSTINE

TO LIONEL JOHNSON

To the Rose upon the Rood of Time

Red Rose, proud Rose, sad Rose of all my days!
Come near me, while I sing the ancient ways:
Cuchulain[2] *battling with the bitter tide;*
The Druid, gray, wood-nurtured, quiet-eyed,
Who cast round Fergus[3] *dreams, and ruin untold;*
And thine own sadness, whereof stars, grown old
In dancing silver sandalled on the sea,
Sing in their high and lonely melody.
Come near, that no more blinded by man's fate,
I find under the boughs of love and hate,
In all poor foolish things that live a day,
Eternal beauty wandering on her way.

Come near, come near, come near—Ah, leave me still
A little space for the rose-breath to fill!
Lest I no more hear common things that crave;
The weak worm hiding down in its small cave,
The field mouse running by me in the grass,
And heavy mortal hopes that toil and pass;
But seek alone to hear the strange things said
By God to the bright hearts of those long dead,
And learn to chaunt a tongue men do not know.
Come near; I would, before my time to go,
Sing of old Eire and the ancient ways:
Red Rose, proud Rose, sad Rose of all my days.

---

[1] "Too late I loved you, Beauty so old and so new! Too late I loved you."
[2] An Irish hero of the Red Branch (or Ulster) cycle of tales.
[3] A king of Ulster; another figure from the Red Branch cycle.

Fergus and the Druid

FERGUS

The whole day have I followed in the rocks,
And you have changed and flowed from shape to shape.
First as a raven on whose ancient wings
Scarcely a feather lingered, then you seemed
A weasel moving on from stone to stone,
And now at last you wear a human shape,
A thin gray man half lost in gathering night.

DRUID

What would you, king of the proud Red Branch kings?

FERGUS

This would I say, most wise of living souls:
Young subtle Concobar[1] sat close by me
When I gave judgment, and his words were wise,
And what to me was burden without end,
To him seemed easy, so I laid the crown
Upon his head to cast away my care.

DRUID

What would you, king of the proud Red Branch kings?

FERGUS

I feast amid my people on the hill,
And pace the woods, and drive my chariot wheels
In the white border of the murmuring sea;
And still I feel the crown upon my head.

DRUID

What would you?

FERGUS

                    I would be no more a king,
But learn the dreaming wisdom that is yours.

---

[1] Stepson of Fergus, later King of Ulster.

DRUID

Look on my thin gray hair and hollow cheeks,
And on these hands that may not lift the sword,
This body trembling like a wind-blown reed.
No woman loves me, no man seeks my help,
Because I be not of the things I dream.

FERGUS

A wild and foolish labourer is a king,
To do and do and do, and never dream.

DRUID

Take, if you must, this little bag of dreams;
Unloose the cord, and they will wrap you round.

FERGUS

I see my life go dripping like a stream
From change to change; I have been many things,
A green drop in the surge, a gleam of light
Upon a sword, a fir-tree on a hill,
An old slave grinding at a heavy quern,
A king sitting upon a chair of gold,
And all these things were wonderful and great;
But now I have grown nothing, being all,
And the whole world weighs down upon my heart:
Ah! Druid, Druid, how great webs of sorrow
Lay hidden in the small slate-coloured bag!

The Death of Cuchulain

A man came slowly from the setting sun,
To Forgail's daughter, Emer,[1] in her dun,
And found her dyeing cloth with subtle care,
And said, casting aside his draggled hair:
"I am Aleel, the swineherd, whom you bid
"Go dwell upon the sea cliffs, vapour hid;
"But now my years of watching are no more."

---

[1] Cuchulain's wife.

Then Emer cast the web upon the floor,
And stretching out her arms, red with the dye,
Parted her lips with a loud sudden cry.

Looking on her, Aleel, the swineherd, said:
"Not any god alive, nor mortal dead,
"Has slain so mighty armies, so great kings,
"Nor won the gold that now Cuchulain brings."

"Why do you tremble thus from feet to crown?"

Aleel, the swineherd, wept and cast him down
Upon the web-heaped floor, and thus his word:
"With him is one sweet-throated like a bird."

"Who bade you tell these things?" and then she cried
To those about, "Beat him with thongs of hide
"And drive him from the door."

      And thus it was:
And where her son, Finmole, on the smooth grass
Was driving cattle, came she with swift feet,
And called out to him, "Son, it is not meet
"That you stay idling here with flocks and herds."

"I have long waited, mother, for those words:
"But wherefore now?"

      "There is a man to die;
"You have the heaviest arm under the sky."

"My father dwells among the sea-worn bands,
"And breaks the ridge of battle with his hands."

"Nay, you are taller than Cuchulain, son."

"He is the mightiest man in ship or dun."

"Nay, he is old and sad with many wars,
"And weary of the crash of battle cars."

"I only ask what way my journey lies,
"For God, who made you bitter, made you wise."

"The Red Branch kings a tireless banquet keep,
"Where the sun falls into the Western deep.
"Go there, and dwell on the green forest rim;
"But tell alone your name and house to him

"Whose blade compels, and bid them send you one
"Who has a like vow from their triple dun."

Between the lavish shelter of a wood
And the gray tide, the Red Branch multitude
Feasted, and with them old Cuchulain dwelt,
And his young dear one close beside him knelt,
And gazed upon the wisdom of his eyes,
More mournful than the depth of starry skies,
And pondered on the wonder of his days;
And all around the harp-string told his praise,
And Concobar, the Red Branch king of kings,
With his own fingers touched the brazen strings.
At last Cuchulain spake, "A young man strays
"Driving the deer along the woody ways.
"I often hear him singing to and fro,
"I often hear the sweet sound of his bow,
"Seek out what man he is."

                              One went and came.
"He bade me let all know he gives his name
"At the sword point, and bade me bring him one
"Who had a like vow from our triple dun."

"I only of the Red Branch hosted now,"
Cuchulain cried, "have made and keep that vow."

After short fighting in the leafy shade,
He spake to the young man, "Is there no maid
"Who loves you, no white arms to wrap you round,
"Or do you long for the dim sleepy ground,
"That you come here to meet this ancient sword?"

"The dooms of men are in God's hidden hoard."

"Your head a while seemed like a woman's head
"That I loved once."

                         Again the fighting sped,
But now the war rage in Cuchulain woke,
And through the other's shield his long blade broke,
And pierced him.
                         "Speak before your breath is done."

"I am Finmole, mighty Cuchulain's son."

"I put you from your pain. I can no more."

While day its burden on to evening bore,
With head bowed on his knees Cuchulain stayed;
Then Concobar sent that sweet-throated maid,
And she, to win him, his gray hair caressed;
In vain her arms, in vain her soft white breast.
Then Concobar, the subtlest of all men,
Ranking his Druids round him ten by ten,
Spake thus, "Cuchulain will dwell there and brood,
"For three days more in dreadful quietude,
"And then arise, and raving slay us all.
"Go, cast on him delusions magical,
"That he might fight the waves of the loud sea."
And ten by ten under a quicken tree,
The Druids chaunted, swaying in their hands
Tall wands of alder, and white quicken wands.

In three days' time, Cuchulain with a moan
Stood up, and came to the long sands alone:
For four days warred he with the bitter tide;
And the waves flowed above him, and he died.

The Rose of the World

Who dreamed that beauty passes like a dream?
For these red lips, with all their mournful pride,
Mournful that no new wonder may betide,
Troy passed away in one high funeral gleam,
And Usna's children[1] died.

We and the labouring world are passing by:
Amid men's souls, that waver and give place,
Like the pale waters in their wintry race,
Under the passing stars, foam of the sky,
Lives on this lonely face.

Bow down, archangels, in your dim abode:
Before you were, or any hearts to beat,
Weary and kind one lingered by His seat;
He made the world to be a grassy road
Before her wandering feet.

---

[1] Naoise, Ainle and Ardan; they were executed by Conchubar (Concobar).

The Rose of Peace

If Michael, leader of God's host
When Heaven and Hell are met,
Looked down on you from Heaven's door-post
He would his deeds forget.

Brooding no more upon God's wars
In his Divine homestead,
He would go weave out of the stars
A chaplet for your head.

And all folk seeing him bow down,
And white stars tell your praise,
Would come at last to God's great town,
Led on by gentle ways;

And God would bid His warfare cease.
Saying all things were well;
And softly make a rosy peace,
A peace of Heaven with Hell.

The Rose of Battle

Rose of all Roses, Rose of all the World!
The tall thought-woven sails, that flap unfurled
Above the tide of hours, trouble the air,
And God's bell buoyed to be the water's care;
While hushed from fear, or loud with hope, a band
With blown, spray-dabbled hair gather at hand.
Turn if you may from battles never done,
I call, as they go by me one by one,
Danger no refuge holds, and war no peace,
For him who hears love sing and never cease,
Beside her clean-swept hearth, her quiet shade:
But gather all for whom no love hath made
A woven silence, or but came to cast
A song into the air, and singing past
To smile on the pale dawn; and gather you
Who have sought more than is in rain or dew

Or in the sun and moon, or on the earth,
Or sighs amid the wandering, starry mirth,
Or comes in laughter from the sea's sad lips;
And wage God's battles in the long gray ships.
The sad, the lonely, the insatiable,
To these Old Night shall all her mystery tell;
God's bell has claimed them by the little cry
Of their sad hearts, that may not live nor die.

Rose of all Roses, Rose of all the World!
You, too, have come where the dim tides are hurled
Upon the wharves of sorrow, and heard ring
The bell that calls us on; the sweet far thing.
Beauty grown sad with its eternity
Made you of us, and of the dim gray sea.
Our long ships loose thought-woven sails and wait,
For God has bid them share an equal fate;
And when at last defeated in His wars,
They have gone down under the same white stars,
We shall no longer hear the little cry
Of our sad hearts, that may not live nor die.

A Faery Song

Sung by the people of faery over Diarmuid and Grania,[1] who lay in their
bridal sleep under a Cromlech.

We who are old, old and gay,
O so old!
Thousands of years, thousands of years,
If all were told:

Give to these children, new from the world,
Silence and love;
And the long dew-dropping hours of the night,
And the stars above:

Give to these children, new from the world,
Rest far from men.

---

[1] Lovers in the Fenian cycle of tales; Diarmuid was killed by Finn for having eloped with his future bride.

Is anything better, anything better?
Tell us it then:

Us who are old, old and gay,
O so old!
Thousands of years, thousands of years,
If all were told.

The Lake Isle of Innisfree

I will arise and go now, and go to Innisfree,
And a small cabin build there, of clay and wattles made:
Nine bean rows will I have there, a hive for the honey bee,
And live alone in the bee-loud glade.

And I shall have some peace there, for peace comes dropping slow,
Dropping from the veils of the morning to where the cricket sings;
There midnight's all a glimmer, and noon a purple glow,
And evening full of the linnet's wings.

I will arise and go now, for always night and day
I hear lake water lapping with low sounds by the shore;
While I stand on the roadway, or on the pavements gray,
I hear it in the deep heart's core.

A Cradle Song

The angels are stooping
Above your bed;
They weary of trooping
With the whimpering dead.

God's laughing in heaven
To see you so good;
The Shining Seven
Are gay with His mood.

I kiss you and kiss you,
My pigeon, my own;

Ah, how I shall miss you
When you have grown.

The Pity of Love

A pity beyond all telling
Is hid in the heart of love:
The folk who are buying and selling
The clouds on their journey above
The cold wet winds ever blowing
And the shadowy hazel grove
Where mouse-gray waters are flowing
Threaten the head that I love.

The Sorrow of Love

The quarrel of the sparrows in the eaves,
The full round moon and the star-laden sky,
And the loud song of the ever-singing leaves,
Had hid away earth's old and weary cry.

And then you came with those red mournful lips,
And with you came the whole of the world's tears
And all the trouble of her labouring ships,
And all the trouble of her myriad years.

And now the sparrows warring in the eaves,
The curd-pale moon, the white stars in the sky,
And the loud chaunting of the unquiet leaves,
Are shaken with earth's old and weary cry.

When You Are Old

When you are old and gray and full of sleep,
And nodding by the fire, take down this book,
And slowly read, and dream of the soft look
Your eyes had once, and of their shadows deep;

How many loved your moments of glad grace,
And loved your beauty with love false or true;
But one man loved the pilgrim soul in you,
And loved the sorrows of your changing face.

And bending down beside the glowing bars
Murmur, a little sadly, how love fled
And paced upon the mountains overhead
And hid his face amid a crowd of stars.

The White Birds

I would that we were, my beloved, white birds on the foam of the
    sea!
We tire of the flame of the meteor, before it can fade and flee;
And the flame of the blue star of twilight, hung low on the rim of the
    sky,
Has awaked in our hearts, my beloved, a sadness that may not die.

A weariness comes from those dreamers, dew dabbled, the lily and
    rose;
Ah, dream not of them, my beloved, the flame of the meteor that
    goes,
Or the flame of the blue star that lingers hung low in the fall of the
    dew:
For I would we were changed to white birds on the wandering foam:
    I and you!

I am haunted by numberless islands, and many a Danaan[1] shore,
Where Time would surely forget us, and Sorrow come near us no
    more;
Soon far from the rose and the lily, and fret of the flames would we
    be,
Were we only white birds, my beloved, buoyed out on the foam of
    the sea!

A Dream of Death

I dreamed that one had died in a strange place
Near no accustomed hand;

---

[1] Fairy.

And they had nailed the boards above her face
The peasants of that land,
And, wondering, planted by her solitude
A cypress and a yew:
I came, and wrote upon a cross of wood
Man had no more to do:
She was more beautiful than thy first love,
This lady by the trees:
And gazed upon the mournful stars above,
And heard the mournful breeze.

A Dream of a Blessed Spirit

All the heavy days are over;
Leave the body's coloured pride
Underneath the grass and clover,
With the feet laid side by side.

One with her are mirth and duty,
Bear the gold embroidered dress,
For she needs not her sad beauty,
To the scented oaken press.

Hers the kiss of Mother Mary,
The long hair is on her face;
Still she goes with footsteps wary,
Full of earth's old timid grace.

With white feet of angels seven
Her white feet go glimmering
And above the deep of heaven,
Flame on flame and wing on wing.

Who Goes with Fergus?

Who will go drive with Fergus now,
And pierce the deep wood's woven shade,
And dance upon the level shore?

Young man, lift up your russet brow,
And lift your tender eyelids, maid,
And brood on hopes and fears no more.

And no more turn aside and brood
Upon Love's bitter mystery;
For Fergus rules the brazen cars,
And rules the shadows of the wood,
And the white breast of the dim sea
And all dishevelled wandering stars.

The Man Who Dreamed of Faeryland

He stood among a crowd at Drumahair;
His heart hung all upon a silken dress,
And he had known at last some tenderness,
Before earth made of him her sleepy care;
But when a man poured fish into a pile,
It seemed they raised their little silver heads,
And sang how day a Druid twilight sheds
Upon a dim, green, well-beloved isle,
Where people love beside star-laden seas;
How Time may never mar their faery vows
Under the woven roofs of quicken boughs:
The singing shook him out of his new ease.

He wandered by the sands of Lisadill;
His mind ran all on money cares and fears,
And he had known at last some prudent years
Before they heaped his grave under the hill;
But while he passed before a plashy place,
A lug-worm with its gray and muddy mouth
Sang how somewhere to north or west or south
There dwelt a gay, exulting, gentle race;
And how beneath those three times blessed skies
A Danaan fruitage makes a shower of moons,
And as it falls awakens leafy tunes:
And at that singing he was no more wise.

He mused beside the well of Scanavin,
He mused upon his mockers: without fail

His sudden vengeance were a country tale,
Now that deep earth has drunk his body in;
But one small knot-grass growing by the pool
Told where, ah, little, all-unneeded voice!
Old Silence bids a lonely folk rejoice,
And chaplet their calm brows with leafage cool,
And how, when fades the sea-strewn rose of day,
A gentle feeling wraps them like a fleece,
And all their trouble dies into its peace:
The tale drove his fine angry mood away.

He slept under the hill of Lugnagall;
And might have known at last unhaunted sleep
Under that cold and vapour-turbaned steep,
Now that old earth had taken man and all:
Were not the worms that spired about his bones
A-telling with their low and reedy cry,
Of how God leans His hands out of the sky,
To bless that isle with honey in His tones;
That none may feel the power of squall and wave
And no one any leaf-crowned dancer miss
Until He burn up Nature with a kiss:
The man has found no comfort in the grave.

The Dedication to a Book of Stories Selected from the Irish Novelists

There was a green branch hung with many a bell
When her own people ruled in wave-worn Eire;
And from its murmuring greenness, calm of faery,
A Druid kindness, on all hearers fell.

It charmed away the merchant from his guile,
And turned the farmer's memory from his cattle,
And hushed in sleep the roaring ranks of battle,
For all who heard it dreamed a little while.

Ah, Exiles wandering over many seas,
Spinning at all times Eire's good to-morrow!
Ah, worldwide Nation, always growing Sorrow!
I also bear a bell branch full of ease.

I tore it from green boughs winds tossed and hurled,
Green boughs of tossing always, weary, weary!
I tore it from the green boughs of old Eire,
The willow of the many-sorrowed world.

Ah, Exiles, wandering over many lands!
My bell branch murmurs: the gay bells bring laughter,
Leaping to shake a cobweb from the rafter;
The sad bells bow the forehead on the hands.

A honeyed ringing: under the new skies
They bring you memories of old village faces;
Cabins gone now, old well-sides, old dear places;
And men who loved the cause that never dies.

The Lamentation of the Old Pensioner

I had a chair at every hearth,
When no one turned to see,
With "Look at that old fellow there,
"And who may he be?"
And therefore do I wander now,
And the fret lies on me.

The road-side trees keep murmuring
Ah, wherefore murmur ye,
As in the old days long gone by,
Green oak and poplar tree?
The well-known faces are all gone
And the fret lies on me.

The Ballad of Father Gilligan

The old priest Peter Gilligan
Was weary night and day;
For half his flock were in their beds,
Or under green sods lay.

Once, while he nodded on a chair,
At the moth-hour of eve,
Another poor man sent for him,
And he began to grieve.

"I have no rest, nor joy, nor peace,
"For people die and die";
And after cried he, "God forgive!
"My body spake, not I!"

He knelt, and leaning on the chair
He prayed and fell asleep;
And the moth-hour went from the fields,
And stars began to peep.

They slowly into millions grew,
And leaves shook in the wind;
And God covered the world with shade,
And whispered to mankind.

Upon the time of sparrow chirp
When the moths came once more,
The old priest Peter Gilligan
Stood upright on the floor.

"Mavrone,[1] mavrone! the man has died,
"While I slept on the chair";
He roused his horse out of its sleep,
And rode with little care.

He rode now as he never rode,
By rocky lane and fen;
The sick man's wife opened the door:
"Father! you come again!"

"And is the poor man dead?" he cried.
"He died an hour ago,"
The old priest Peter Gilligan
In grief swayed to and fro.

"When you were gone, he turned and died
"As merry as a bird."

---

[1] A cry of lamentation.

The old priest Peter Gilligan
He knelt him at that word.

"He who hath made the night of stars
"For souls, who tire and bleed,
"Sent one of His great angels down
"To help me in my need.

"He who is wrapped in purple robes,
"With planets in His care,
"Had pity on the least of things
"Asleep upon a chair."

The Two Trees

Beloved, gaze in thine own heart,
The holy tree is growing there;
From joy the holy branches start,
And all the trembling flowers they bear.
The changing colours of its fruit
Have dowered the stars with merry light;
The surety of its hidden root
Has planted quiet in the night;
The shaking of its leafy head
Has given the waves their melody,
And made my lips and music wed,
Murmuring a wizard song for thee.
There, through bewildered branches, go
Winged Loves borne on in gentle strife,
Tossing and tossing to and fro
The flaming circle of our life.
When looking on their shaken hair,
And dreaming how they dance and dart,
Thine eyes grow full of tender care:
Beloved, gaze in thine own heart.

Gaze no more in the bitter glass
The demons, with their subtle guile,
Lift up before us when they pass,
Or only gaze a little while;

For there a fatal image grows,
With broken boughs, and blackened leaves,
And roots half hidden under snows
Driven by a storm that ever grieves.
For all things turn to barrenness
In the dim glass the demons hold,
The glass of outer weariness,
Made when God slept in times of old.
There, through the broken branches, go
The ravens of unresting thought;
Peering and flying to and fro
To see men's souls bartered and bought.
When they are heard upon the wind,
And when they shake their wings; alas!
Thy tender eyes grow all unkind:
Gaze no more in the bitter glass.

To Some I Have Talked with by the Fire

While I wrought out these fitful Danaan rhymes,
My heart would brim with dreams about the times
When we bent down above the fading coals;
And talked of the dark folk, who live in souls
Of passionate men, like bats in the dead trees;
And of the wayward twilight companies,
Who sigh with mingled sorrow and content,
Because their blossoming dreams have never bent
Under the fruit of evil and of good:
And of the embattled flaming multitude
Who rise, wing above wing, flame above flame,
And, like a storm, cry the Ineffable Name,
And with the clashing of their sword blades make
A rapturous music, till the morning break,
And the white hush end all, but the loud beat
Of their long wings, the flash of their white feet.

To Ireland in the Coming Times

Know, that I would accounted be
True brother of that company,
Who sang to sweeten Ireland's wrong,
Ballad and story, rann[1] and song;
Nor be I any less of them,
Because the red-rose-bordered hem
Of her, whose history began
Before God made the angelic clan,
Trails all about the written page;
For in the world's first blossoming age
The light fall of her flying feet
Made Ireland's heart begin to beat;
And still the starry candles flare
To help her light foot here and there;
And still the thoughts of Ireland brood
Upon her holy quietude.

Nor may I less be counted one
With Davis, Mangan, Ferguson,[2]
Because to him, who ponders well,
My rhymes more than their rhyming tell
Of the dim wisdoms old and deep,
That God gives unto man in sleep.
For the elemental beings go
About my table to and fro.
In flood and fire and clay and wind,
They huddle from man's pondering mind;
Yet he who treads in austere ways
May surely meet their ancient gaze.
Man ever journeys on with them
After the red-rose-bordered hem.
Ah, faeries, dancing under the moon,
A Druid land, a Druid tune!

---

[1] Verse.
[2] Nineteenth-century Irish writers.

While still I may, I write for you
The love I lived, the dream I knew.
From our birthday, until we die,
Is but the winking of an eye;
And we, our singing and our love,
The mariners of night above,
And all the wizard things that go
About my table to and fro,
Are passing on to where may be,
In truth's consuming ecstasy
No place for love and dream at all;
For God goes by with white foot-fall.
I cast my heart into my rhymes,
That you, in the dim coming times,
May know how my heart went with them
After the red-rose-bordered hem.

THE WIND AMONG THE REEDS

The Hosting of the Sidhe[1]

The host is riding from Knocknarea
And over the grave of Clooth-na-bare;
Caolte tossing his burning hair
And Niamh[2] calling *Away, come away:*
Empty your heart of its mortal dream.
The winds awaken, the leaves whirl round,
Our cheeks are pale, our hair is unbound,
Our breasts are heaving, our eyes are a-gleam,
Our arms are waving, our lips are apart;
And if any gaze on our rushing band,
We come between him and the deed of his hand,
We come between him and the hope of his heart.
The host is rushing 'twixt night and day,
And where is there hope or deed as fair?
Caolte tossing his burning hair,
And Niamh calling *Away, come away.*

The Everlasting Voices

O sweet everlasting Voices, be still;
Go to the guards of the heavenly fold
And bid them wander obeying your will,
Flame under flame, till Time be no more;
Have you not heard that our hearts are old,
That you call in birds, in wind on the hill,
In shaken boughs, in tide on the shore?
O sweet everlasting Voices, be still.

---

[1] Ancient Irish gods, the Tribes of the goddess Danu.
[2] Caolte and Niamh (a beautiful woman) were among the Sidhe.

The Moods

Time drops in decay,
Like a candle burnt out,
And the mountains and woods
Have their day, have their day;
What one in the rout
Of the fire-born moods
Has fallen away?

Aedh[1] Tells of the Rose in His Heart

All things uncomely and broken, all things worn out and old,
The cry of a child by the roadway, the creak of a lumbering cart,
The heavy steps of the ploughman, splashing the wintry mould,
Are wronging your image that blossoms a rose in the deeps of my
     heart.

The wrong of unshapely things is a wrong too great to be told;
I hunger to build them anew and sit on a green knoll apart,
With the earth and the sky and the water, remade, like a casket of
     gold
For my dreams of your image that blossoms a rose in the deeps of
     my heart.

The Host of the Air

O'Driscoll drove with a song
The wild duck and the drake
From the tall and the tufted reeds
Of the drear Hart Lake.

And he saw how the reeds grew dark
At the coming of night tide,

---

[1] Aedh, along with Hanrahan and Michael Robartes, is a figure in Yeats's book of stories
The Secret Rose (1897).

And dreamed of the long dim hair
Of Bridget his bride.

He heard while he sang and dreamed
A piper piping away,
And never was piping so sad,
And never was piping so gay.

And he saw young men and young girls
Who danced on a level place,
And Bridget his bride among them,
With a sad and a gay face.

The dancers crowded about him,
And many a sweet thing said,
And a young man brought him red wine
And a young girl white bread.

But Bridget drew him by the sleeve,
Away from the merry bands,
To old men playing at cards
With a twinkling of ancient hands.

The bread and the wine had a doom,
For these were the host of the air;
He sat and played in a dream
Of her long dim hair.

He played with the merry old men
And thought not of evil chance,
Until one bore Bridget his bride
Away from the merry dance.

He bore her away in his arms,
The handsomest young man there,
And his neck and his breast and his arms
Were drowned in her long dim hair.

O'Driscoll scattered the cards
And out of his dream awoke:
Old men and young men and young girls
Were gone like a drifting smoke;

But he heard high up in the air
A piper piping away,

And never was piping so sad,
And never was piping so gay.

Breasal the Fisherman

Although you hide in the ebb and flow
Of the pale tide when the moon has set,
The people of coming days will know
About the casting out of my net,
And how you have leaped times out of mind
Over the little silver cords,
And think that you were hard and unkind,
And blame you with many bitter words.

A Cradle Song

The Danaan children laugh, in cradles of wrought gold,
And clap their hands together, and half close their eyes,
For they will ride the North when the ger-eagle flies,
With heavy whitening wings, and a heart fallen cold:
I kiss my wailing child and press it to my breast,
And hear the narrow graves calling my child and me.
Desolate winds that cry over the wandering sea;
Desolate winds that hover in the flaming West;
Desolate winds that beat the doors of Heaven, and beat
The doors of Hell and blow there many a whimpering ghost;
O heart the winds have shaken, the unappeasable host
Is comelier than candles before Maurya's[1] feet.

Into the Twilight

Out-worn heart, in a time out-worn,
Come clear of the nets of wrong and right;

---

[1] The Virgin Mary.

Laugh, heart, again in the gray twilight,
Sigh, heart, again in the dew of the morn.

Your mother Eire is always young,
Dew ever shining and twilight gray;
Though hope fall from you and love decay,
Burning in fires of a slanderous tongue.

Come, heart, where hill is heaped upon hill:
For there the mystical brotherhood
Of sun and moon and hollow and wood
And river and stream work out their will;

And God stands winding His lonely horn,
And time and the world are ever in flight;
And love is less kind than the gray twilight,
And hope is less dear than the dew of the morn.

The Song of Wandering Aengus

I went out to the hazel wood,
Because a fire was in my head,
And cut and peeled a hazel wand,
And hooked a berry to a thread;
And when white moths were on the wing,
And moth-like stars were flickering out,
I dropped the berry in a stream
And caught a little silver trout.

When I had laid it on the floor
I went to blow the fire a-flame,
But something rustled on the floor,
And someone called me by my name:
It had become a glimmering girl
With apple blossom in her hair
Who called me by my name and ran
And faded through the brightening air.

Though I am old with wandering
Through hollow lands and hilly lands,
I will find out where she has gone,
And kiss her lips and take her hands;

And walk among long dappled grass,
And pluck till time and times are done
The silver apples of the moon,
The golden apples of the sun.

The Song of the Old Mother

I rise in the dawn, and I kneel and blow
Till the seed of the fire flicker and glow;
And then I must scrub and bake and sweep
Till stars are beginning to blink and peep;
And the young lie long and dream in their bed
Of the matching of ribbons for bosom and head,
And their day goes over in idleness,
And they sigh if the wind but lift a tress:
While I must work because I am old,
And the seed of the fire gets feeble and cold.

The Fiddler of Dooney

When I play on my fiddle in Dooney,
Folk dance like a wave of the sea;
My cousin is priest in Kilvarnet,
My brother in Moharabuiee.

I passed my brother and cousin:
They read in their books of prayer;
I read in my book of songs
I bought at the Sligo fair.

When we come at the end of time
To Peter sitting in state,
He will smile on the three old spirits,
But call me first through the gate;

For the good are always the merry,
Save by an evil chance,
And the merry love the fiddle
And the merry love to dance:

And when the folk there spy me,
They will all come up to me,
With 'Here is the fiddler of Dooney!'
And dance like a wave of the sea.

The Heart of the Woman

O what to me the little room
That was brimmed up with prayer and rest;
He bade me out into the gloom,
And my breast lies upon his breast.

O what to me my mother's care,
The house where I was safe and warm;
The shadowy blossom of my hair
Will hide us from the bitter storm.

O hiding hair and dewy eyes,
I am no more with life and death,
My heart upon his warm heart lies,
My breath is mixed into his breath.

Aedh Laments the Loss of Love

Pale brows, still hands and dim hair,
I had a beautiful friend
And dreamed that the old despair
Would end in love in the end:
She looked in my heart one day
And saw your image was there;
She has gone weeping away.

Mongan[1] Laments the Change That Has Come upon Him and His Beloved

Do you not hear me calling, white deer with no horns?
I have been changed to a hound with one red ear;

---

[1] A legendary Irish sorcerer and king.

I have been in the Path of Stones and the Wood of Thorns,
For somebody hid hatred and hope and desire and fear
Under my feet that they follow you night and day.
A man with a hazel wand came without sound;
He changed me suddenly; I was looking another way;
And now my calling is but the calling of a hound;
And Time and Birth and Change are hurrying by.
I would that the boar without bristles had come from the West
And had rooted the sun and moon and stars out of the sky
And lay in the darkness, grunting, and turning to his rest.

Michael Robartes Bids His Beloved Be at Peace

I hear the Shadowy Horses, their long manes a-shake,
Their hoofs heavy with tumult, their eyes glimmering white;
The North unfolds above them clinging, creeping night,
The East her hidden joy before the morning break,
The West weeps in pale dew and sighs passing away,
The South is pouring down roses of crimson fire:
O vanity of Sleep, Hope, Dream, endless Desire,
The Horses of Disaster plunge in the heavy clay:
Beloved, let your eyes half close, and your heart beat
Over my heart, and your hair fall over my breast,
Drowning love's lonely hour in deep twilight of rest,
And hiding their tossing manes and their tumultuous feet.

Hanrahan Reproves the Curlew

O curlew, cry no more in the air,
Or only to the waters in the West;
Because your crying brings to my mind
Passion-dimmed eyes and long heavy hair
That was shaken out over my breast:
There is enough evil in the crying of wind.

Michael Robartes Remembers Forgotten Beauty

When my arms wrap you round I press
My heart upon the loveliness

That has long faded from the world;
The jewelled crowns that kings have hurled
In shadowy pools, when armies fled;
The love-tales wove with silken thread
By dreaming ladies upon cloth
That has made fat the murderous moth;
The roses that of old time were
Woven by ladies in their hair,
The dew-cold lilies ladies bore
Through many a sacred corridor
Where such gray clouds of incense rose
That only gods' eyes did not close:
For that pale breast and lingering hand
Come from a more dream-heavy land,
A more dream-heavy hour than this;
And when you sigh from kiss to kiss
I hear white Beauty sighing, too,
For hours when all must fade like dew,
But flame on flame, deep under deep,
Throne over throne, where in half sleep,
Their swords upon their iron knees,
Brood her high lonely mysteries.

A Poet to His Beloved

I bring you with reverent hands
The books of my numberless dreams,
White woman that passion has worn
As the tide wears the dove-gray sands,
And with heart more old than the horn
That is brimmed from the pale fire of time:
White woman with numberless dreams,
I bring you my passionate rhyme.

Aedh Gives His Beloved Certain Rhymes

Fasten your hair with a golden pin,
And bind up every wandering tress;
I bade my heart build these poor rhymes:

It worked at them, day out, day in,
Building a sorrowful loveliness
Out of the battles of old times.

You need but lift a pearl-pale hand,
And bind up your long hair and sigh;
And all men's hearts must burn and beat;
And candle-like foam on the dim sand,
And stars climbing the dew-dropping sky,
Live but to light your passing feet.

To My Heart, Bidding It Have No Fear

Be you still, be you still, trembling heart;
Remember the wisdom out of the old days:
Him who trembles before the flame and the flood,
And the winds that blow through the starry ways,
Let the starry winds and the flame and the flood
Cover over and hide, for he has no part
With the proud, majestical multitude.

The Cap and Bells

The jester walked in the garden:
The garden had fallen still;
He bade his soul rise upward
And stand on her window-sill.

It rose in a straight blue garment,
When owls began to call:
It had grown wise-tongued by thinking
Of a quiet and light footfall;

But the young queen would not listen;
She rose in her pale night gown;
She drew in the heavy casement
And pushed the latches down.

He bade his heart go to her,
When the owls called out no more;

In a red and quivering garment
It sang to her through the door.

It had grown sweet-tongued by dreaming
Of a flutter of flower-like hair;
But she took up her fan from the table
And waved it off on the air.

'I have cap and bells,' he pondered,
'I will send them to her and die';
And when the morning whitened
He left them where she went by.

She laid them upon her bosom,
Under a cloud of her hair,
And her red lips sang them a love song
Till stars grew out of the air.

She opened her door and her window,
And the heart and the soul came through,
To her right hand came the red one,
To her left hand came the blue.

They set up a noise like crickets,
A chattering wise and sweet,
And her hair was a folded flower
And the quiet of love in her feet.

The Valley of the Black Pig

The dews drop slowly and dreams gather: unknown spears
Suddenly hurtle before my dream-awakened eyes,
And then the clash of fallen horsemen and the cries
Of unknown perishing armies beat about my ears.
We who still labour by the cromlech on the shore,
The gray cairn on the hill, when day sinks drowned in dew,
Being weary of the world's empires, bow down to you,
Master of the still stars and of the flaming door.

Michael Robartes Asks Forgiveness Because of His Many Moods

If this importunate heart trouble your peace
With words lighter than air,
Or hopes that in mere hoping flicker and cease;
Crumple the rose in your hair;
And cover your lips with odorous twilight and say,
'O Hearts of wind-blown flame!
'O Winds, elder than changing of night and day,
'That murmuring and longing came
'From marble cities loud with tabors of old
'In dove-gray faery lands;
'From battle banners, fold upon purple fold,
'Queens wrought with glimmering hands;
'That saw young Niamh hover with love-lorn face
'Above the wandering tide;
'And lingered in the hidden desolate place
'Where the last Phœnix died,
'And wrapped the flames above his holy head;
'And still murmur and long:
'O Piteous Hearts, changing till change be dead
'In a tumultuous song':
And cover the pale blossoms of your breast
With your dim heavy hair,
And trouble with a sigh for all things longing for rest
The odorous twilight there.

Aedh Tells of a Valley Full of Lovers

I dreamed that I stood in a valley, and amid sighs,
For happy lovers passed two by two where I stood;
And I dreamed my lost love came stealthily out of the wood
With her cloud-pale eyelids falling on dream-dimmed eyes:
I cried in my dream, *'O women, bid the young men lay*
'Their heads on your knees, and drown their eyes with your hair,
'Or remembering hers they will find no other face fair
'Till all the valleys of the world have been withered away.'

Aedh Tells of the Perfect Beauty

O cloud-pale eyelids, dream-dimmed eyes,
The poets labouring all their days
To build a perfect beauty in rhyme
Are overthrown by a woman's gaze
And by the unlabouring brood of the skies:
And therefore my heart will bow, when dew
Is dropping sleep, until God burn time,
Before the unlabouring stars and you.

Aedh Hears the Cry of the Sedge

I wander by the edge
Of this desolate lake
Where wind cries in the sedge:
Until the axle break
That keeps the stars in their round,
And hands hurl in the deep
The banners of East and West,
And the girdle of light is unbound,
Your breast will not lie by the breast
Of your beloved in sleep.

Aedh Thinks of Those Who Have Spoken Evil of His Beloved

Half close your eyelids, loosen your hair,
And dream about the great and their pride;
They have spoken against you everywhere,
But weigh this song with the great and their pride;
I made it out of a mouthful of air,
Their children's children shall say they have lied.

The Blessed

Cumhal called out, bending his head,
Till Dathi came and stood,

With a blink in his eyes, at the cave mouth,
Between the wind and the wood.

And Cumhal said, bending his knees,
'I have come by the windy way
'To gather the half of your blessedness
'And learn to pray when you pray.

'I can bring you salmon out of the streams
'And heron out of the skies.'
But Dathi folded his hands and smiled
With the secrets of God in his eyes.

And Cumhal saw like a drifting smoke
All manner of blessed souls,
Women and children, young men with books,
And old men with croziers and stoles.

'Praise God and God's mother,' Dathi said,
'For God and God's mother have sent
'The blessedest souls that walk in the world
'To fill your heart with content.'

'And which is the blessedest,' Cumhal said,
'Where all are comely and good?
'Is it these that with golden thuribles
'Are singing about the wood?'

'My eyes are blinking,' Dathi said,
'With the secrets of God half blind,
'But I can see where the wind goes
'And follow the way of the wind;

'And blessedness goes where the wind goes,
'And when it is gone we are dead;
'I see the blessedest soul in the world
'And he nods a drunken head.

'O blessedness comes in the night and the day
'And whither the wise heart knows;
'And one has seen in the redness of wine
'The Incorruptible Rose,

'That drowsily drops faint leaves on him
'And the sweetness of desire,

'While time and the world are ebbing away
'In twilights of dew and of fire.'

The Secret Rose

Far off, most secret, and inviolate Rose,
Enfold me in my hour of hours; where those
Who sought thee in the Holy Sepulchre,
Or in the wine vat, dwell beyond the stir
And tumult of defeated dreams; and deep
Among pale eyelids, heavy with the sleep
Men have named beauty. Thy great leaves enfold
The ancient beards, the helms of ruby and gold
Of the crowned Magi; and the king whose eyes
Saw the Pierced Hands and Rood of elder rise
In druid vapour and make the torches dim;
Till vain frenzy awoke and he died; and him
Who met Fand[1] walking among flaming dew
By a gray shore where the wind never blew,
And lost the world and Emer for a kiss;
And him who drove the gods out of their liss,[2]
And till a hundred morns had flowered red,
Feasted and wept the barrows of his dead;
And the proud dreaming king who flung the crown
And sorrow away, and calling bard and clown
Dwelt among wine-stained wanderers in deep woods;
And him who sold tillage, and house, and goods,
And sought through lands and islands numberless years,
Until he found, with laughter and with tears,
A woman of so shining loveliness
That men threshed corn at midnight by a tress,
A little stolen tress. I, too, await
The hour of thy great wind of love and hate.
When shall the stars be blown about the sky,
Like the sparks blown out of a smithy, and die?
Surely thine hour has come, thy great wind blows,
Far off, most secret, and inviolate Rose?

---

[1] Wife of the god of the sea.
[2] Mound.

Hanrahan Laments Because of His Wanderings

O where is our Mother of Peace
Nodding her purple hood?
For the winds that awakened the stars
Are blowing through my blood.
I would that the death-pale deer
Had come through the mountain side,
And trampled the mountain away,
And drunk up the murmuring tide;
For the winds that awakened the stars
Are blowing through my blood,
And our Mother of Peace has forgot me
Under her purple hood.

The Travail of Passion

When the flaming lute-thronged angelic door is wide;
When an immortal passion breathes in mortal clay;
Our hearts endure the scourge, the plaited thorns, the way
Crowded with bitter faces, the wounds in palm and side,
The hyssop-heavy sponge, the flowers by Kidron stream;[1]
We will bend down and loosen our hair over you,
That it may drop faint perfume, and be heavy with dew,
Lilies of death-pale hope, roses of passionate dream.

The Poet Pleads with His Friend for Old Friends

Though you are in your shining days,
Voices among the crowd
And new friends busy with your praise,
Be not unkind or proud,
But think about old friends the most:
Time's bitter flood will rise,
Your beauty perish and be lost
For all eyes but these eyes.

---

[1] Kidron (or Kedron) flows between the Mount of Olives and Jerusalem.

Hanrahan Speaks to the Lovers of His Songs in Coming Days

O colleens, [1] kneeling by your altar rails long hence,
When songs I wove for my beloved hide the prayer,
And smoke from this dead heart drifts through the violet air
And covers away the smoke of myrrh and frankincense;
Bend down and pray for the great sin I wove in song,
Till Maurya of the wounded heart cry a sweet cry,
And call to my beloved and me: 'No longer fly
'Amid the hovering, piteous, penitential throng.'

Aedh Pleads with the Elemental Powers

The Powers whose name and shape no living creature knows
Have pulled the Immortal Rose;
And though the Seven Lights bowed in their dance and wept,
The Polar Dragon slept,
His heavy rings uncoiled from glimmering deep to deep:
When will he wake from sleep?

Great Powers of falling wave and wind and windy fire,
With your harmonious choir
Encircle her I love and sing her into peace,
That my old care may cease;
Unfold your flaming wings and cover out of sight
The nets of day and night.

Dim Powers of drowsy thought, let her no longer be
Like the pale cup of the sea,
When winds have gathered and sun and moon burned dim
Above its cloudy rim;
But let a gentle silence wrought with music flow
Whither her footsteps go.

---

[1] Girls.

Aedh Wishes His Beloved Were Dead

Were you but lying cold and dead,
And lights were paling out of the West,
You would come hither, and bend your head,
And I would lay my head on your breast;
And you would murmur tender words,
Forgiving me, because you were dead:
Nor would you rise and hasten away,
Though you have the will of the wild birds,
But know your hair was bound and wound
About the stars and moon and sun:
O would, beloved, that you lay
Under the dock-leaves in the ground,
While lights were paling one by one.

Aedh Wishes for the Cloths of Heaven

Had I the heavens' embroidered cloths,
Enwrought with golden and silver light,
The blue and the dim and the dark cloths
Of night and light and the half-light,
I would spread the cloths under your feet:
But I, being poor, have only my dreams;
I have spread my dreams under your feet;
Tread softly because you tread on my dreams.

Mongan Thinks of His Past Greatness

I have drunk ale from the Country of the Young[1]
And weep because I know all things now:
I have been a hazel tree, and they hung
The Pilot Star and the Crooked Plough
Among my leaves in times out of mind:
I became a rush that horses tread:

---

[1] The realm of the happy dead.

I became a man, a hater of the wind,
Knowing one, out of all things, alone, that his head
Would not lie on the breast or his lips on the hair
Of the woman that he loves, until he dies;
Although the rushes and the fowl of the air
Cry of his love with their pitiful cries.

IN THE SEVEN WOODS

In the Seven Woods

I have heard the pigeons of the Seven Woods
Make their faint thunder, and the garden bees
Hum in the lime tree flowers; and put away
The unavailing outcries and the old bitterness
That empty the heart. I have forgot awhile
Tara uprooted, and new commonness
Upon the throne and crying about the streets
And hanging its paper flowers from post to post,
Because it is alone of all things happy.
I am contented, for I know that Quiet
Wanders laughing and eating her wild heart
Among pigeons and bees, while that Great Archer,
Who but awaits His hour to shoot, still hangs
A cloudy quiver over Parc-na-Lee.

August 1902

The Arrow

I thought of your beauty, and this arrow,
Made out of a wild thought, is in my marrow.
There's no man may look upon her, no man,
As when newly grown to be a woman,
Blossom pale, she pulled down the pale blossom
At the moth hour and hid it in her bosom.
This beauty's kinder, yet for a reason
I could weep that the old is out of season.

The Folly of Being Comforted

One that is ever kind said yesterday:
'Your well-beloved's hair has threads of grey,

59

To love you in the old high way of love;
That it had all seemed happy, and yet we'd grown
As weary-hearted as that hollow moon.

The Song of Red Hanrahan

The old brown thorn trees break in two high over Cummen Strand
Under a bitter black wind that blows from the left hand,
Our courage breaks like an old tree in a black wind and dies;
But we have hidden in our hearts the flame out of the eyes
Of Cathleen, the daughter of Houlihan. [1]

The wind has bundled up the clouds high over Knocknarea
And thrown the thunder on the stones for all that Maeve[2] can say.
Angers that are like noisy clouds have set our hearts abeat;
But we have all bent low and low and kissed the quiet feet
Of Cathleen, the daughter of Houlihan.

The yellow pool has overflowed high up on Clooth-na-Bare,
For the wet winds are blowing out of the clinging air;
Like heavy flooded waters our bodies and our blood;
But purer than a tall candle before the Holy Rood
Is Cathleen, the daughter of Houlihan.

The Old Men Admiring Themselves in the Water

I heard the old, old men say,
'Everything alters,
And one by one we drop away.'
They had hands like claws, and their knees
Were twisted like the old thorn trees
By the waters.
I heard the old, old men say,
'All that's beautiful drifts away
Like the waters.'

---

[1] An allegorical name for Ireland.
[2] Queen of Connacht.

Under the Moon

I have no happiness in dreaming of Brycelinde,[1]
Nor Avalon the grass-green hollow, nor Joyous Isle,
Where one found Lancelot crazed and hid him for a while,
Nor Ulad,[2] when Naoise had thrown a sail upon the wind,
Nor lands that seem too dim to be burdens on the heart,
Land-under-Wave, where out of the moon's light and the sun's
Seven old sisters wind the threads of the long-lived ones,
Land-of-the-Tower, where Aengus has thrown the gates apart,
And Wood-of-Wonders, where one kills an ox at dawn
To find it when night falls laid on a golden bier:
Therein are many queens like Branwen, and Guinivere;
And Niam, and Laban,[3] and Fand, who could change to an otter or
        fawn,
And the wood-woman whose lover was changed to a blue-eyed
        hawk;
And whether I go in my dreams by woodland, or dun, or shore,
Or on the unpeopled waves with kings to pull at the oar,
I hear the harpstring praise them or hear their mournful talk.
Because of a story I heard under the thin horn
Of the third moon, that hung between the night and the day,
To dream of women whose beauty was folded in dismay,
Even in an old story, is a burden not to be borne.

The Players Ask for a Blessing on the Psalteries and
Themselves

THREE VOICES TOGETHER
Hurry to bless the hands that play,
The mouths that speak, the notes and strings,
O masters of the glittering town!
O! lay the shrilly trumpet down,
Though drunken with the flags that sway

---

[1] The forest in which Merlin was bewitched by Viviane.
[2] Ulster.
[3] Fand's sister.

Over the ramparts and the towers,
And with the waving of your wings.

FIRST VOICE
Maybe they linger by the way;
One gathers up his purple gown;
One leans and mutters by the wall;
He dreads the weight of mortal hours.

SECOND VOICE
O no, O no, they hurry down
Like plovers that have heard the call.

THIRD VOICE
O kinsmen of the Three in One,
O kinsmen, bless the hands that play.
The notes they waken shall live on
When all this heavy history's done.
Our hands, our hands must ebb away.

THREE VOICES TOGETHER
The proud and careless notes live on,
But bless our hands that ebb away.

The Rider from the North

There's many a strong farmer
Whose heart would break in two
If he could see the townland
That we are riding to;
Boughs have their fruit and blossom
At all times of the year,
Rivers are running over
With red beer and brown beer.
An old man plays the bagpipes
In a golden and silver wood,
Queens, their eyes blue like the ice,
Are dancing in a crowd.

The little fox he murmured,
'O what is the world's bane?'
The sun was laughing sweetly,

The moon plucked at my rein;
But the little red fox murmured,
'O do not pluck at his rein,
He is riding to the townland
That is the world's bane.'

When their hearts are so high
That they would come to blows,
They unhook their heavy swords
From golden and silver boughs;
But all that are killed in battle
Awaken to life again;
It is lucky that their story
Is not known among men.
For O, the strong farmers
That would let the spade lie,
For their hearts would be like a cup
That somebody had drunk dry.

The little fox he murmured,
'O what is the world's bane?'
The sun was laughing sweetly,
The moon plucked at my rein;
But the little red fox murmured,
'O do not pluck at his rein,
He is riding to the townland
That is the world's bane.'

Michael will unhook his trumpet
From a bough overhead,
And blow a little noise
When the supper has been spread.
Gabriel will come from the water
With a fish tail, and talk
Of wonders that have happened
On wet roads where men walk,
And lift up an old horn
Of hammered silver, and drink
Till he has fallen asleep
Upon the starry brink.

The little fox he murmured,
'O what is the world's bane?'

The sun was laughing sweetly,
The moon plucked at my rein;
But the little red fox murmured,
'O do not pluck at his rein,
He is riding to the townland
That is the world's bane.'

THE GREEN HELMET AND OTHER POEMS

His Dream

I swayed upon the gaudy stern
The butt end of a steering oar,
And everywhere that I could turn
Men ran upon the shore.

And though I would have hushed the crowd,
There was no mother's son but said,
'What is the figure in a shroud
Upon a gaudy bed?'

And fishes bubbling to the brim
Cried out upon that thing beneath,
It had such dignity of limb,
By the sweet name of Death.

Though I'd my finger on my lip,
What could I but take up the song?
And fish and crowd and gaudy ship
Cried out the whole night long,

Crying amid the glittering sea,
Naming it with ecstatic breath,
Because it had such dignity,
By the sweet name of Death.

A Woman Homer Sung

If any man drew near
When I was young,
I thought, 'He holds her dear,'
And shook with hate and fear.
But oh, 'twas bitter wrong,
If he could pass her by
With an indifferent eye.

Whereon I wrote and wrought
And now, being grey,
I dream that I have brought
To such a pitch my thought
That coming time can say,
'He shadowed in a glass
What thing her body was.'

For she had fiery blood
When I was young,
And trod so sweetly proud
As 'twere upon a cloud,
A woman Homer sung,
That life and letters seem
But an heroic dream.

The Consolation

I had this thought a while ago,
My darling cannot understand
What I have done, or what would do
In this blind bitter land;

And I grew weary of the sun
Until my thoughts cleared up again,
Remembering that the best I have done
Was done to make it plain;

That every year I have cried, 'At length
My darling understands it all,
Because I have come into my strength,
And words obey my call';

That had she done so who can say
What would have shaken from the sieve?
I might have thrown poor words away
And been content to live.

No Second Troy

Why should I blame her that she filled my days
With misery, or that she would of late

Have taught to ignorant men most violent ways,
Or hurled the little streets upon the great,
Had they but courage equal to desire?
What could have made her peaceful with a mind
That nobleness made simple as a fire,
With beauty like a tightened bow, a kind
That is not natural in an age like this,
Being high and solitary and most stern?
Why, what could she have done, being what she is?
Was there another Troy for her to burn?

Reconciliation

Some may have blamed you that you took away
The verses that they cared for on the day
When, the ears being deafened, the sight of the eyes blind
With lightning, you went from me, and I could find
Nothing to make a song about but kings,
Helmets, and swords, and half-forgotten things
That were like memories of you—but now
We'll out, for the world lives as long ago;
And while we're in our laughing, weeping fit,
Hurl helmets, crowns, and swords into the pit.
But, dear, cling close to me; since you were gone,
My barren thoughts have chilled me to the bone.

King and No King

'Would it were anything but merely voice!'
The NO King cried who after that was King,
Because he had not heard of anything
That balanced with a word is more than noise;
Yet Old Romance being kind, let him prevail
Somewhere or somehow that I have forgot,
Though he'd but cannon—Whereas we that had thought
To have lit upon as clean and sweet a tale
Have been defeated by that pledge you gave

In momentary anger long ago;
And I that have not your faith, how shall I know
That in the blinding light beyond the grave
We'll find so good a thing as that we have lost?
The hourly kindness, the day's common speech,
The habitual content of each with each
When neither soul nor body has been crossed.

Peace

Ah, that Time could touch a form
That could show what Homer's age
Bred to be a hero's wage.
'Were not all her life but storm,
Would not painters paint a form
Of such noble lines,' I said,
'Such a delicate high head,
So much sternness and such charm?'
Ah, but peace that comes at length,
Came when Time had touched her form.

Against Unworthy Praise

Oh, heart, be at peace, because
Nor knave nor dolt can break
What's not for their applause,
Being for a woman's sake.
Enough if the work has seemed,
So did she your strength renew,
A dream that a lion had dreamed
Till the wilderness cried aloud,
A secret between you two,
Between the proud and the proud.

What, still you would have their praise!
But here's a haughtier text,
The labyrinth of her days
That her own strangeness perplexed.
And how what her dreaming gave

Earned slander, ingratitude,
From self-same dolt and knave;
Ay, and worse wrong than these.
Yet she, singing upon her road,
Half lion, half child, is at peace.

The Fascination of What's Difficult

The fascination of what's difficult
Has dried the sap out of my veins, and rent
Spontaneous joy and natural content
Out of my heart. There's something ails our colt
That must, as if it had not holy blood,
Nor on an Olympus leaped from cloud to cloud,
Shiver under the lash, strain, sweat, and jolt
As though it dragged road metal. My curse on plays
That have to be set up in fifty ways,
On the day's war with every knave and dolt,
Theatre business, management of men.
I swear before the dawn comes round again
I'll find the stable and pull out the bolt.

A Drinking Song

Wine comes in at the mouth
And love comes in at the eye;
That's all we shall know for truth
Before we grow old and die.
I lift the glass to my mouth,
I look at you, and I sigh.

The Coming of Wisdom with Time

Though leaves are many, the root is one;
Through all the lying days of my youth
I swayed my leaves and flowers in the sun;
Now I may wither into the truth.

To a Poet, Who Would Have Me Praise Certain Bad Poets, Imitators of His and of Mine

You say, as I have often given tongue
In praise of what another's said or sung,
'Twere politic to do the like by these,
But where's the wild dog that has praised his fleas?

A Lyric from an Unpublished Play

'Put off that mask of burning gold
With emerald eyes.'
'O no, my dear, you make so bold
To find if hearts be wild and wise,
And yet not cold.'

'I would but find what's there to find,
Love or deceit.'
'It was the mask engaged your mind,
And after set your heart to beat,
Not what's behind.'

'But lest you are my enemy,
I must enquire.'
'O no, my dear, let all that be,
What matter, so there is but fire
In you, in me?'

Upon a Threatened House

How should the world be luckier if this house,
Where passion and precision have been one
Time out of mind, became too ruinous
To breed the lidless eye that loves the sun?
And the sweet laughing eagle thoughts that grow

Where wings have memory of wings, and all
That comes of the best knit to the best? although
Mean roof-trees were the sturdier for its fall.
How should their luck run high enough to reach
The gifts that govern men, and after these
To gradual Time's last gift, a written speech
Wrought of high laughter, loveliness and ease?

These Are the Clouds

These are the clouds about the fallen sun,
The majesty that shuts his burning eye;
The weak lay hand on what the strong has done,
Till that be tumbled that was lifted high
And discord follow upon unison,
And all things at one common level lie.
And therefore, friend, if your great race were run
And these things came, so much the more thereby
Have you made greatness your companion,
Although it be for children that you sigh:
These are the clouds about the fallen sun,
The majesty that shuts his burning eye.

At Galway Races

Out yonder, where the Race Course is,
Delight makes all of the one mind,
The riders upon the swift horses,
The field that closes in behind:
We too had good attendance once,
Hearers and hearteners of the work;
Aye, horsemen for companions,
Before the merchant and the clerk
Breathed on the world with timid breath.
Sing on: sometime, and at some new moon

We'll learn that sleeping is not death,
Hearing the whole earth change its tune,
Its flesh being wild, and it again
Crying aloud as the race course is,
And we find hearteners among men
That ride upon horses.

A Friend's Illness

Sickness brought me this
Thought, in that scale of his:
Why should I be dismayed
Though flame had burned the whole
World, as it were a coal,
Now I have seen it weighed
Against a soul?

All Things Can Tempt Me

All things can tempt me from this craft of verse,
One time it was a woman's face, or worse,
The seeming needs of my fool-driven land;
Now nothing but comes readier to the hand
Than this accustomed toil. When I was young,
I had not given a penny for a song
Did not the poet sing it with such airs
That one believed he had a sword upstairs,
Yet would be now, could I but have my wish,
Colder and dumber and deafer than a fish.

The Young Man's Song

I whispered, 'I am too young,'
And then, 'I am old enough,'
Wherefore I threw a penny

To find out if I might love;
'Go and love, go and love, young man,
If the lady be young and fair,'
Ah, penny, brown penny, brown penny,
I am looped in the loops of her hair.

Oh, love is the crooked thing,
There is nobody wise enough
To find out all that is in it,
For he would be thinking of love
Till the stars had run away,
And the shadows eaten the moon;
Ah, penny, brown penny, brown penny,
One cannot begin it too soon.

RESPONSIBILITIES

'In dreams begins responsibility.'
OLD PLAY

'How am I fallen from myself, for a long time now
I have not seen the Prince of Chang in my dreams.'
KHOUNG-FOU-TSEU[1]

Pardon, old fathers, if you still remain
Somewhere in ear-shot for the story's end,
Old Dublin merchant 'free of ten and four'
Or trading out of Galway into Spain;
And country scholar, Robert Emmet's[2] friend,
A hundred-year-old memory to the poor;
Traders or soldiers who have left me blood
That has not passed through any huxter's loin,
Pardon, and you that did not weigh the cost,
Old Butlers when you took to horse and stood
Beside the brackish waters of the Boyne
Till your bad master blenched and all was lost;
And merchant skipper that leaped overboard
After a ragged hat in Biscay Bay;
You most of all, silent and fierce old man,
Because you were the spectacle that stirred
My fancy, and set my boyish lips to say,
'Only the wasteful virtues earn the sun';
Pardon that for a barren passion's sake,
Although I have come close on forty-nine,
I have no child, I have nothing but a book,
Nothing but that to prove your blood and mine.

January 1914

---

[1] Confucius.
[2] An Irish patriot, executed in 1803.

The Grey Rock

Poets with whom I learned my trade,
Companions of the Cheshire Cheese,[1]
Here's an old story I've re-made,
Imagining 'twould better please
Your ears than stories now in fashion,
Though you may think I waste my breath
Pretending that there can be passion
That has more life in it than death,
And though at bottling of your wine
The bow-legged Goban[2] *had no say;*
The moral's yours because it's mine.

When cups went round at close of day—
Is not that how good stories run?—
Somewhere within some hollow hill
If books speak truth, in Slievenamon,
But let that be, the gods were still
And sleepy, having had their meal,
And smoky torches made a glare
On painted pillars, on a deal
Of fiddles and of flutes hung there
By the ancient holy hands that brought them
From murmuring Murias, on cups—
Old Goban hammered them and wrought them,
And put his pattern round their tops
To hold the wine they buy of him.

But from the juice that made them wise
All those had lifted up the dim
Imaginations of their eyes,
For one that was like woman made
Before their sleepy eyelids ran
And trembling with her passion said,
'Come out and dig for a dead man,
Who's burrowing somewhere in the ground,

---

[1] Inn frequented by Samuel Johnson, here referring to the Rhymers' Club, to which Yeats belonged.
[2] An ancient Irish god.

And mock him to his face and then
Hollo him on with horse and hound,
For he is the worst of all dead men.'

We should be dazed and terror-struck,
If we but saw in dreams that room,
Those wine-drenched eyes, and curse our luck
That emptied all our days to come.
I knew a woman none could please,
Because she dreamed when but a child
Of men and women made like these;
And after, when her blood ran wild,
Had ravelled her own story out,
And said, 'In two or in three years
I needs must marry some poor lout,'
And having said it, burst in tears.
Since, tavern comrades, you have died,
Maybe your images have stood,
Mere bone and muscle thrown aside,
Before that roomful or as good.
You had to face your ends when young—
'Twas wine or women, or some curse—
But never made a poorer song
That you might have a heavier purse,
Nor gave loud service to a cause
That you might have a troop of friends.
You kept the Muses' sterner laws,
And unrepenting faced your ends,
And therefore earned the right—and yet
Dowson and Johnson[1] *most I praise—*
To troop with those the world's forgot,
And copy their proud steady gaze.

'The Danish troop was driven out
Between the dawn and dusk,' she said;
'Although the event was long in doubt,
Although the King of Ireland's dead
And half the kings, before sundown
All was accomplished.

                    'When this day

---

[1] Ernest Dowson and Lionel Johnson, members of the Rhymers' Club.

Murrough, the King of Ireland's son,
Foot after foot was giving way,
He and his best troops back to back
Had perished there, but the Danes ran,
Stricken with panic from the attack,
The shouting of an unseen man;
And being thankful Murrough found,
Led by a footsole dipped in blood
That had made prints upon the ground,
Where by old thorn trees that man stood;
And though when he gazed here and there,
He had but gazed on thorn trees, spoke,
"Who is the friend that seems but air
And yet could give so fine a stroke?"
Thereon a young man met his eye,
Who said, "Because she held me in
Her love, and would not have me die,
Rock-nurtured Aoife[1] took a pin,
And pushing it into my shirt,
Promised that for a pin's sake
No man should see to do me hurt;
But there it's gone; I will not take
The fortune that had been my shame
Seeing, King's son, what wounds you have."
'Twas roundly spoke, but when night came
He had betrayed me to his grave,
For he and the King's son were dead.
I'd promised him two hundred years,
And when for all I'd done or said—
And these immortal eyes shed tears—
He claimed his country's need was most,
I'd saved his life, yet for the sake
Of a new friend he has turned a ghost.
What does he care if my heart break?
I call for spade and horse and hound
That we may harry him.' Thereon
She cast herself upon the ground
And rent her clothes and made her moan:
'Why are they faithless when their might

---

[1] A warrior-queen of Scotland; also an Irish goddess.

Is from the holy shades that rove
The grey rock and the windy light?
Why should the faithfullest heart most love
The bitter sweetness of false faces?
Why must the lasting love what passes,
Why are the gods by men betrayed?'

But thereon every god stood up
With a slow smile and without sound,
And stretching forth his arm and cup
To where she moaned upon the ground,
Suddenly drenched her to the skin;
And she with Goban's wine adrip,
No more remembering what had been,
Stared at the gods with laughing lip.

I have kept my faith, though faith was tried,
To that rock-born, rock-wandering foot,
And the world's altered since you died,
And I am in no good repute
With the loud host before the sea,
That think sword strokes were better meant
Than lover's music—let that be,
So that the wandering foot's content.

To a Wealthy Man Who Promised a Second Subscription to the Dublin Municipal Gallery if It Were Proved the People Wanted Pictures

You gave, but will not give again
Until enough of Paudeen's pence
By Biddy's[1] halfpennies have lain
To be 'some sort of evidence,'
Before you'll put your guineas down,
That things it were a pride to give
Are what the blind and ignorant town
Imagines best to make it thrive.
What cared Duke Ercole,[2] that bid

---

[1] The crowd; "Paudeen" has the same meaning.
[2] A fifteenth-century Italian duke and patron of the arts.

His mummers to the market place,
What th' onion-sellers thought or did
So that his Plautus set the pace
For the Italian comedies?
And Guidobaldo,[1] when he made
That grammar school of courtesies
Where wit and beauty learned their trade
Upon Urbino's windy hill,
Had sent no runners to and fro
That he might learn the shepherds' will.
And when they drove out Cosimo,[2]
Indifferent how the rancour ran,
He gave the hours they had set free
To Michelozzo's[3] latest plan
For the San Marco Library,
Whence turbulent Italy should draw
Delight in Art whose end is peace,
In logic and in natural law
By sucking at the dugs of Greece.

Your open hand but shows our loss,
For he knew better how to live.
Let Paudeens play at pitch and toss,
Look up in the sun's eye and give
What the exultant heart calls good
That some new day may breed the best
Because you gave, not what they would,
But the right twigs for an eagle's nest!

December 1912

September 1913

What need you, being come to sense,
But fumble in a greasy till
And add the halfpence to the pence
And prayer to shivering prayer, until

---

[1] A fifteenth-century Italian duke.
[2] Cosimo de' Medici, a fifteenth-century Florentine politician.
[3] A Florentine architect.

You have dried the marrow from the bone?
For men were born to pray and save,
Romantic Ireland's dead and gone,
It's with O'Leary[1] in the grave.

Yet they were of a different kind,
The names that stilled your childish play,
They have gone about the world like wind,
But little time had they to pray
For whom the hangman's rope was spun,
And what, God help us, could they save?
Romantic Ireland's dead and gone,
It's with O'Leary in the grave.

Was it for this the wild geese spread
The grey wing upon every tide;
For this that all that blood was shed,
For this Edward Fitzgerald[2] died,
And Robert Emmet and Wolfe Tone,[3]
All that delirium of the brave?
Romantic Ireland's dead and gone,
It's with O'Leary in the grave.

Yet could we turn the years again,
And call those exiles as they were,
In all their loneliness and pain,
You'd cry, 'Some woman's yellow hair
Has maddened every mother's son':
They weighed so lightly what they gave,
But let them be, they're dead and gone,
They're with O'Leary in the grave.

To a Friend Whose Work Has Come to Nothing

Now all the truth is out,
Be secret and take defeat
From any brazen throat,

---

[1] John O'Leary (1830–1907), an Irish patriot and friend of Yeats's father.

[2] A member of the United Irishmen; he died in 1798 from wounds received during his arrest.

[3] Founder of the United Irish Club; he committed suicide in prison, in 1798.

For how can you compete,
Being honour bred, with one
Who, were it proved he lies,
Were neither shamed in his own
Nor in his neighbours' eyes?
Bred to a harder thing
Than Triumph, turn away
And like a laughing string
Whereon mad fingers play
Amid a place of stone,
Be secret and exult,
Because of all things known
That is most difficult.

Paudeen

Indignant at the fumbling wits, the obscure spite
Of our old Paudeen in his shop, I stumbled blind
Among the stones and thorn trees, under morning light,
Until a curlew cried and in the luminous wind
A curlew answered, and I was startled by the thought
That on the lonely height where all are in God's eye,
There cannot be, confusion of our sound forgot,
A single soul that lacks a sweet crystalline cry.

To a Shade

If you[1] have revisited the town, thin Shade,
Whether to look upon your monument
(I wonder if the builder has been paid)
Or happier-thoughted when the day is spent
To drink of that salt breath out of the sea
When grey gulls flit about instead of men,
And the gaunt houses put on majesty:
Let these content you and be gone again;
For they are at their old tricks yet.

---

[1] The Irish nationalist leader Charles Stewart Parnell (1846–1891).

A man
Of your own passionate serving kind who had brought
In his full hands what, had they only known,
Had given their children's children loftier thought,
Sweeter emotion, working in their veins
Like gentle blood, has been driven from the place,
And insult heaped upon him for his pains
And for his open-handedness, disgrace;
An old foul mouth that once cried out on you,
Herding the pack.

Unquiet wanderer,
Draw the Glasnevin coverlet anew
About your head till the dust stops your ear,
The time for you to taste of that salt breath
And listen at the corners has not come;
You had enough of sorrow before death—
Away, away! You are safer in the tomb.

September 29th, 1913

When Helen Lived

We have cried in our despair
That men desert,
For some trivial affair
Or noisy, insolent sport,
Beauty that we have won
From bitterest hours;
Yet we, had we walked within
Those topless towers
Where Helen walked with her boy,
Had given but as the rest
Of the men and women of Troy,
A word and a jest.

The Attack on 'The Playboy of the Western World,' 1907

Once, when midnight smote the air,
Eunuchs ran through Hell and met

Round about Hell's Gate to stare
Upon great Juan riding by;
And like these to rail and sweat
Staring on his sinewy thigh.

The Three Beggars

'Though to my feathers in the wet,
I have stood here from break of day,
I have not found a thing to eat,
For only rubbish comes my way.
Am I to live on lebeen-lone?'[1]
Muttered the old crane of Gort.
'For all my pains on lebeen-lone?'

King Guari[2] walked amid his court,
The palace-yard and river-side
And there to three old beggars said:
'You that have wandered far and wide
Can ravel out what's in my head.
Do men who least desire get most,
Or get the most who most desire?'
A beggar said: 'They get the most
Whom man or devil cannot tire,
And what could make their muscles taut
Unless desire had made them so?'
But Guari laughed with secret thought,
'If that be true as it seems true,
One of you three is a rich man,
For he shall have a thousand pounds
Who is first asleep, if but he can
Sleep before the third noon sounds.'
And thereon, merry as a bird,
With his old thoughts King Guari went
From river-side and palace-yard
And left them to their argument.
'And if I win,' one beggar said,

---

[1] (?) Fish food.
[2] A seventh-century king of Connacht.

'Though I am old I shall persuade
A pretty girl to share my bed';
The second, 'I shall learn a trade';
The third, 'I'll hurry to the course
Among the other gentlemen,
And lay it all upon a horse.'
'But now that I have thought again,
There is a solid dignity
About a farm,' the second cried.

The exorbitant dreams of beggary,
That idleness had borne to pride,
Sang through their teeth from noon to noon;
And when the second twilight brought
The frenzy of the beggars' moon
They closed their blood-shot eyes for naught.
One beggar cried: 'You're shamming sleep,'
And thereupon their anger grew,
Till they were whirling in a heap.

They'd mauled and bitten the night through
Or sat upon their heels to rail,
And when old Guari came and stood
Before the three to end this tale,
They were commingling lice and blood.
'Time's up,' he cried, and all the three
With blood-shot eyes upon him stared.
'Time's up,' he cried, and all the three
Fell down upon the dust and snored.

'Maybe I shall be lucky yet,
Now they are silent,' said the crane.
'Though to my feathers in the wet,
I've stood as I were made of stone
And seen the rubbish run about,
It's certain there are trout somewhere
And maybe I shall take a trout
If but I do not seem to care.'

The Three Hermits

Three old hermits took the air
By a cold and desolate sea,
First was muttering a prayer,
Second rummaged for a flea;
On a windy stone, the third,
Giddy with his hundredth year,
Sang unnoticed like a bird:
'Though the Door of Death is near
And what waits behind the door,
Three times in a single day
I, though upright on the shore,
Fall asleep when I should pray.'
So the first, but now the second:
'We're but given what we have earned
When all thoughts and deeds are reckoned,
So it's plain to be discerned
That the shades of holy men
Who have failed, being weak of will,
Pass the Door of Birth again,
And are plagued by crowds, until
They've the passion to escape.'
Moaned the other, 'They are thrown
Into some most fearful shape.'
But the second mocked his moan:
'They are not changed to anything,
Having loved God once, but maybe
To a poet or a king
Or a witty lovely lady.'
While he'd rummaged rags and hair,
Caught and cracked his flea, the third,
Giddy with his hundredth year,
Sang unnoticed like a bird.

Beggar to Beggar Cried

'Time to put off the world and go somewhere
And find my health again in the sea air,'

Beggar to beggar cried, being frenzy-struck,
'And make my soul before my pate is bare.'

'And get a comfortable wife and house
To rid me of the devil in my shoes,'
Beggar to beggar cried, being frenzy-struck,
'And the worse devil that is between my thighs.'

'And though I'd marry with a comely lass,
She need not be too comely—let it pass,'
Beggar to beggar cried, being frenzy-struck,
'But there's a devil in a looking-glass.'

'Nor should she be too rich, because the rich
Are driven by wealth as beggars by the itch,'
Beggar to beggar cried, being frenzy-struck,
'And cannot have a humorous happy speech.'

'And there I'll grow respected at my ease,
And hear amid the garden's nightly peace,'
Beggar to beggar cried, being frenzy-struck,
'The wind-blown clamour of the barnacle-geese.'

Running to Paradise

As I came over Windy Gap
They threw a halfpenny into my cap,
For I am running to Paradise.
And all that I need do is to wish
And somebody puts his hand in the dish
To throw me a bit of salted fish:
And there the king is but as the beggar.

My brother Mourteen is worn out
With skelping[1] his big brawling lout,
And I am running to Paradise.
A poor life, do what he can,
And though he keep a dog and a gun,
A serving maid and a serving man:
And there the king is but as the beggar.

---

[1] Beating.

Poor men have grown to be rich men,
And rich men grown to be poor again,
While I am running to Paradise.
And many a darling wit's grown dull
That tossed a bare heel when at school,
Now it has filled an old sock full:
And there the king is but as the beggar.

The wind is old and still at play
While I must hurry upon my way,
For I am running to Paradise.
Yet never have I lit on a friend
To take my fancy like the wind
That nobody can buy or bind:
And there the king is but as the beggar.

The Hour Before Dawn

A one-legged, one-armed, one-eyed man,
A bundle of rags upon a crutch,
Stumbled as windy Cruachan,
Cursing the wind. It was as much
As the one sturdy leg could do
To keep him upright while he cursed.
He counted, where long years ago
Queen Maeve's nine Maines[1] had been nursed,
A pair of lapwings, one old sheep
And not a house to the plain's edge,
When close to his right hand a heap
Of grey stones and a rocky ledge
Reminded him that he could make,
If he but shifted a few stones,
A shelter till the daylight broke.
But while he fumbled with the stones
They toppled over; 'Were it not
I have a lucky wooden shin
I had been hurt,' the old beggar thought,
And thereon saw, where stones had been,

---

[1] Maeve's sons.

A dark deep hole in the rock's face,
Trembled and gasped and should have run,
Being certain it was no right place,
But the Hell Mouth at Cruachan
And stuffed with all that's old and bad;
And yet stood still, because inside
He had seen a red-haired jolly lad
In some outlandish coat beside
A ladle and a tub of beer,
Plainly no phantom by his look;
So with a laugh at his own fear
He crawled into that pleasant nook.
Young Red-head stretched himself to yawn
And murmured 'May God curse the night
That's grown uneasy near the dawn
So that it seems even I sleep light;
And who are you that wakens me?
Has one of Maeve's nine brawling sons
Grown tired of his own company?
But let him keep his grave for once,
I have to find the sleep I have lost.'
And then at last, being wide awake,
'I took you for a brawling ghost,
Say what you please, but from day-break
I'll sleep another century.'
The beggar, deaf to all but hope,
Went down upon a hand and knee
And took the wooden ladle up
And would have dipped it in the beer,
But the other pushed his hand aside;
'Before you have dipped it in the beer
That sacred Goban brewed,' he cried,
'I'll have my say, till I am able
To judge if a light-sleeping fool
Would have his fill out of my ladle
To make a clatter in the hole
In the bad hour before dawn.
You've but to drink the beer and say
I'll sleep until the winter's gone,
Or maybe to Midsummer's Day,
And so it will be. At the first
I waited so for that or this—

Because the weather was a-cursed
Or I'd no woman there to kiss,
And slept for half a year or so;
But year by year I found that less
Gave me such pleasure I'd forgo
Even a half hour's nothingness,
And when at one year's end I found
I had not waked a single minute,
I chose this burrow under ground
And sleep away all Time within it.
My sleep were now nine centuries
But for those mornings when I find
The lapwing at their foolish cries
And the sheep bleating at the wind
As when I also played the fool.'

The beggar in a rage began
Upon his hunkers in the hole,
'It's plain that you are no right man
To mock at everything I love
As if it were not worth the doing.
I'd have a merry life enough
If a good Easter wind were blowing,
And though the winter wind is bad
I should not be too down in the mouth
For anything you did or said
If but this wind were in the south.'

But the other cried, 'You long for the spring
Or that the wind would shift a point,
And do not know that you would bring,
If time were suppler in the joint,
Neither the spring nor the south wind
But the hour when you shall pass away
And leave no smoking wick behind,
For all life longs for the Last Day
And there's no man but cocks his ear
To know when Michael's trumpet cries
That flesh and bone may disappear,
And souls as if they were but sighs,
And there be nothing but God left;
But I alone being blessed keep

Like some old rabbit to my cleft
And wait Him in a drunken sleep.'
He dipped his ladle in the tub
And drank and yawned and stretched him out.

The other shouted, 'You would rob
My life of every pleasant thought
And every comfortable thing,
And so take that and that.' Thereon
He gave him a great pummelling,
But might have pummelled at a stone
For all the sleeper knew or cared;
And after heaped the stones again,
And cursed and prayed, and prayed and cursed
'Oh God if he get loose!' And then
In fury and in panic fled
From the Hell Mouth at Cruachan,
And gave God thanks that overhead
The clouds were brightening with the dawn.

The Player Queen
(Song from an Unfinished Play)

My mother dandled me and sang,
'How young it is, how young!'
And made a golden cradle
That on a willow swung.

'He went away,' my mother sang,
'When I was brought to bed,'
And all the while her needle pulled
The gold and silver thread.

She pulled the thread and bit the thread
And made a golden gown,
And wept because she had dreamt that I
Was born to wear a crown.

'When she was got,' my mother sang,
'I heard a sea-mew cry,
And saw a flake of the yellow foam
That dropped upon my thigh.'

How therefore could she help but braid
The gold into my hair,
And dream that I should carry
The golden top of care?

The Realists

Hope that you may understand!
What can books of men that wive
In a dragon-guarded land,
Paintings of the dolphin-drawn
Sea-nymphs in their pearly waggons
Do, but awake a hope to live
That had gone
With the dragons?

I. The Witch

Toil and grow rich,
What's that but to lie
With a foul witch
And after, drained dry,
To be brought
To the chamber where
Lies one long sought
With despair?

II. The Peacock

What's riches to him
That has made a great peacock
With the pride of his eye?
The wind-beaten, stone-grey,
And desolate Three-rock
Would nourish his whim.
Live he or die
Amid wet rocks and heather,

His ghost will be gay
Adding feather to feather
For the pride of his eye.

The Mountain Tomb

Pour wine and dance if Manhood still have pride,
Bring roses if the rose be yet in bloom;
The cataract smokes on the mountain side,
Our Father Rosicross is in his tomb.

Pull down the blinds, bring fiddle and clarionet
That there be no foot silent in the room
Nor mouth from kissing, nor from wine unwet;
Our Father Rosicross is in his tomb.

In vain, in vain; the cataract still cries,
The everlasting taper lights the gloom;
All wisdom shut into his onyx eyes,
Our Father Rosicross sleeps in his tomb.

To a Child Dancing in the Wind

I

Dance there upon the shore;
What need have you to care
For wind or water's roar?
And tumble out your hair
That the salt drops have wet;
Being young you have not known
The fool's triumph, nor yet
Love lost as soon as won,
Nor the best labourer dead
And all the sheaves to bind.
What need have you to dread
The monstrous crying of wind?

II

Has no one said those daring
Kind eyes should be more learn'd?
I have found out how despairing

The moths are when they are burned,
But I am old and you are young,
So we speak a different tongue.

O you will take whatever's offered
And dream that all the world's a friend,
Suffer as your mother suffered,
Be as broken in the end.
I could have warned you—but you are young,
And I speak a barbarous tongue.

A Memory of Youth

The moments passed as at a play,
I had the wisdom love brings forth;
I had my share of mother wit
And yet for all that I could say,
And though I had her praise for it,
A cloud blown from the cut-throat north
Suddenly hid love's moon away.

Believing every word I said,
I praised her body and her mind
Till pride had made her eyes grow bright,
And pleasure made her cheeks grow red,
And vanity her footfall light,
Yet we, for all that praise, could find
Nothing but darkness overhead.

We sat as silent as a stone,
We knew, though she'd not said a word,
That even the best of love must die,
And had been savagely undone
Were it not that love upon the cry
Of a most ridiculous little bird
Tore from the clouds his marvellous moon.

Fallen Majesty

Although crowds gathered once if she but showed her face,
And even old men's eyes grew dim, this hand alone,

Like some last courtier at a gypsy camping place,
Babbling of fallen majesty, records what's gone.

The lineaments, a heart that laughter has made sweet,
These, these remain, but I record what's gone. A crowd
Will gather, and not know it walks the very street
Whereon a thing once walked that seemed a burning cloud.

Friends

Now must I these three praise—
Three women that have wrought
What joy is in my days;
One that no thought,
Nor those unpassing cares,
No, not in these fifteen
Many-times-troubled years,
Could ever come between
Heart and delighted heart;
And one because her hand
Had strength that could unbind
What none can understand,
What none can have and thrive,
Youth's dreamy load, till she
So changed me that I live
Labouring in ecstasy.
And what of her that took
All till my youth was gone
With scarce a pitying look?
How should I praise that one?
When day begins to break
I count my good and bad,
Being wakeful for her sake,
Remembering what she had,
What eagle look still shows,
While up from my heart's root
So great a sweetness flows
I shake from head to foot.

The Cold Heaven

Suddenly I saw the cold and rook-delighting Heaven
That seemed as though ice burned and was but the more ice,
And thereupon imagination and heart were driven
So wild that every casual thought of that and this
Vanished, and left but memories, that should be out of season
With the hot blood of youth, of love crossed long ago;
And I took all the blame out of all sense and reason,
Until I cried and trembled and rocked to and fro,
Riddled with light. Ah! when the ghost begins to quicken,
Confusion of the death-bed over, is it sent
Out naked on the roads, as the books say, and stricken
By the injustice of the skies for punishment?

That the Night Come

She lived in storm and strife,
Her soul had such desire
For what proud death may bring
That it could not endure
The common good of life,
But lived as 't were a king
That packed his marriage day
With banneret and pennon,
Trumpet and kettledrum,
And the outrageous cannon,
To bundle time away
That the night come.

An Appointment

Being out of heart with government
I took a broken root to fling
Where the proud, wayward squirrel went,
Taking delight that he could spring;

And he, with that low whinnying sound
That is like laughter, sprang again
And so to the other tree at a bound.
Nor the tame will, nor timid brain,
Bred that fierce tooth and cleanly limb
And threw him up to laugh on the bough;
No government appointed him.

I. The Magi

Now as at all times I can see in the mind's eye,
In their stiff, painted clothes, the pale unsatisfied ones
Appear and disappear in the blue depth of the sky
With all their ancient faces like rain-beaten stones,
And all their helms of silver hovering side by side,
And all their eyes still fixed, hoping to find once more,
Being by Calvary's turbulence unsatisfied,
The uncontrollable mystery on the bestial floor.

II. The Dolls

A doll in the doll-maker's house
Looks at the cradle and bawls:
'That is an insult to us.'
But the oldest of all the dolls,
Who had seen, being kept for show,
Generations of his sort,
Out-screams the whole shelf: 'Although
There's not a man can report
Evil of this place,
The man and the woman bring
Hither, to our disgrace,
A noisy and filthy thing.'
Hearing him groan and stretch
The doll-maker's wife is aware
Her husband has heard the wretch,
And crouched by the arm of his chair,

She murmurs into his ear,
Head upon shoulder leant:
'My dear, my dear, oh dear,
It was an accident.'

A Coat

I made my song a coat
Covered with embroideries
Out of old mythologies
From heel to throat;
But the fools caught it,
Wore it in the world's eye
As though they'd wrought it.
Song, let them take it,
For there's more enterprise
In walking naked.

Alphabetical List of Titles

Alphabetical List of First Lines

DOVER · THRIFT · EDITIONS

All books complete and unabridged. All 5³⁄₁₆″ × 8¼″, paperbound.
Just $1.00 each in U.S.A.

POETRY

BHAGAVADGITA, Bhagavadgita. 112pp. 27782-8

SONGS OF INNOCENCE AND SONGS OF EXPERIENCE, William Blake. 64pp. 27051-3

SONNETS FROM THE PORTUGUESE AND OTHER POEMS, Elizabeth Barrett Browning. 64pp. 27052-1

MY LAST DUCHESS AND OTHER POEMS, Robert Browning. 128pp. 27783-6

POEMS AND SONGS, Robert Burns. 96pp. 26863-2

SELECTED POEMS, George Gordon, Lord Byron. 112pp. 27784-4

THE RIME OF THE ANCIENT MARINER AND OTHER POEMS, Samuel Taylor Coleridge. 80pp. 27266-4

SELECTED POEMS, Emily Dickinson. 64pp. 26466-1

SELECTED POEMS, John Donne. 96pp. 27788-7

THE RUBÁIYÁT OF OMAR KHAYYÁM: FIRST AND FIFTH EDITIONS, Edward FitzGerald. 64pp. 26467-X

A BOY'S WILL AND NORTH OF BOSTON, Robert Frost. 112pp. (Available in U.S. only.) 26866-7

THE ROAD NOT TAKEN AND OTHER POEMS, Robert Frost. 64pp. (Available in U.S. only) 27550-7

A SHROPSHIRE LAD, A. E. Housman. 64pp. 26468-8

LYRIC POEMS, John Keats. 80pp. 26871-3

THE BOOK OF PSALMS, King James Bible. 128pp. 27541-8

GUNGA DIN AND OTHER FAVORITE POEMS, Rudyard Kipling. 80pp. 26471-8

THE CONGO AND OTHER POEMS, Vachel Lindsay. 96pp. 27272-9

FAVORITE POEMS, Henry Wadsworth Longfellow. 96pp. 27273-7

SPOON RIVER ANTHOLOGY, Edgar Lee Masters. 144pp. 27275-3

RENASCENCE AND OTHER POEMS, Edna St. Vincent Millay. 64pp. (Available in U.S. only.) 26873-X

SELECTED POEMS, John Milton. 128pp. 27554-X

THE RAVEN AND OTHER FAVORITE POEMS, Edgar Allan Poe. 64pp. 26685-0

THE SHOOTING OF DAN McGREW AND OTHER POEMS, Robert Service. 96pp. 27556-6

COMPLETE SONGS FROM THE PLAYS, William Shakespeare. 80pp. 27801-8

COMPLETE SONNETS, William Shakespeare. 80pp. 26686-9

SELECTED POEMS, Percy Bysshe Shelley. 128pp. 27558-2

SELECTED POEMS, Alfred, Lord Tennyson. 112pp. 27282-6

CHRISTMAS CAROLS: COMPLETE VERSES, Shane Weller (ed.). 64pp. 27397-0

GREAT LOVE POEMS, Shane Weller (ed.). 128pp. 27284-2

SELECTED POEMS, Walt Whitman. 128pp. 26878-0

THE BALLAD OF READING GAOL AND OTHER POEMS, Oscar Wilde. 64pp. 27072-6

FAVORITE POEMS, William Wordsworth. 80pp. 27073-4

EARLY POEMS, William Butler Yeats. 128pp. 27808-5

DOVER · THRIFT · EDITIONS

All books complete and unabridged. All 5³/₁₆″ × 8¼″, paperbound.
Just $1.00 each in U.S.A.

FICTION

FLATLAND: A ROMANCE OF MANY DIMENSIONS, Edwin A. Abbott. 96pp. 27263-X

BEOWULF, Beowulf (trans. by R. K. Gordon). 64pp. 27264-8

ALICE'S ADVENTURES IN WONDERLAND, Lewis Carroll. 96pp. 27543-4

O PIONEERS!, Willa Cather. 128pp. 27785-2

FIVE GREAT SHORT STORIES, Anton Chekhov. 96pp. 26463-7

FAVORITE FATHER BROWN STORIES, G. K. Chesterton. 96pp. 27545-0

THE AWAKENING, Kate Chopin. 128pp. 27786-0

HEART OF DARKNESS, Joseph Conrad. 80pp. 26464-5

THE SECRET SHARER AND OTHER STORIES, Joseph Conrad. 128pp. 27546-9

THE OPEN BOAT AND OTHER STORIES, Stephen Crane. 128pp. 27547-7

THE RED BADGE OF COURAGE, Stephen Crane. 112pp. 26465-3

A CHRISTMAS CAROL, Charles Dickens. 80pp. 26865-9

NOTES FROM THE UNDERGROUND, Fyodor Dostoyevsky. 96pp. 27053-X

SIX GREAT SHERLOCK HOLMES STORIES, Sir Arthur Conan Doyle. 112pp. 27055-6

WHERE ANGELS FEAR TO TREAD, E. M. Forster. 128pp. (Available in U.S. only) 27791-7

THE OVERCOAT AND OTHER SHORT STORIES, Nikolai Gogol. 112pp. 27057-2

GREAT GHOST STORIES, John Grafton (ed.). 112pp. 27270-2

THE LUCK OF ROARING CAMP AND OTHER SHORT STORIES, Bret Harte. 96pp. 27271-0

YOUNG GOODMAN BROWN AND OTHER SHORT STORIES, Nathaniel Hawthorne. 128pp. 27060-2

THE GIFT OF THE MAGI AND OTHER SHORT STORIES, O. Henry. 96pp. 27061-0

THE NUTCRACKER AND THE GOLDEN POT, E. T. A. Hoffmann. 128pp. 27806-9

THE BEAST IN THE JUNGLE AND OTHER STORIES, Henry James. 128pp. 27552-3

THE TURN OF THE SCREW, Henry James. 96pp. 26684-2

DUBLINERS, James Joyce. 160pp. 26870-5

SELECTED SHORT STORIES, D. H. Lawrence. 128pp. 27794-1

GREEN TEA AND OTHER GHOST STORIES, J. Sheridan LeFanu. 96pp. 27795-X

THE CALL OF THE WILD, Jack London. 64pp. 26472-6

FIVE GREAT SHORT STORIES, Jack London. 96pp. 27063-7

WHITE FANG, Jack London. 160pp. 26968-X

THE NECKLACE AND OTHER SHORT STORIES, Guy de Maupassant. 128pp. 27064-5

BARTLEBY AND BENITO CERENO, Herman Melville. 112pp. 26473-4

THE GOLD-BUG AND OTHER TALES, Edgar Allan Poe. 128pp. 26875-6

THE STRANGE CASE OF DR. JEKYLL AND MR. HYDE, Robert Louis Stevenson. 64pp. 26688-5

TREASURE ISLAND, Robert Louis Stevenson. 160pp. 27559-0

THE KREUTZER SONATA AND OTHER SHORT STORIES, Leo Tolstoy. 144pp. 27805-0

THE MYSTERIOUS STRANGER AND OTHER STORIES, Mark Twain. 128pp. 27069-6

DOVER · THRIFT · EDITIONS

All book ⋯ erbound.

FICTION

CANDIDE, Voltaire (François-Marie Arouet). 112pp. 26689-3
THE INVISIBLE MAN, H. G. Wells. 112pp. (Available in U.S. only.) 27071-8
ETHAN FROME, Edith Wharton. 96pp. 26690-7
THE PICTURE OF DORIAN GRAY, Oscar Wilde. 192pp. 27807-7

NONFICTION

THE DEVIL'S DICTIONARY, Ambrose Bierce. 144pp. 27542-6
SELF-RELIANCE AND OTHER ESSAYS, Ralph Waldo Emerson. 128pp. 27790-9
GREAT SPEECHES, Abraham Lincoln. 112pp. 26872-1
THE PRINCE, Niccolò Machiavelli. 80pp. 27274-5
SYMPOSIUM AND PHAEDRUS, Plato. 96pp. 27798-4
THE TRIAL AND DEATH OF SOCRATES: Four Dialogues, Plato. 128pp. 27066-1
CIVIL DISOBEDIENCE AND OTHER ESSAYS, Henry David Thoreau. 96pp. 27563-9

PLAYS

THE CHERRY ORCHARD, Anton Chekhov. 64pp. 26682-6
THE THREE SISTERS, Anton Chekhov. 64pp. 27544-2
THE WAY OF THE WORLD, William Congreve. 80pp. 27787-9
MEDEA, Euripides. 64pp. 27548-5
THE MIKADO, William Schwenck Gilbert. 64pp. 27268-0
SHE STOOPS TO CONQUER, Oliver Goldsmith. 80pp. 26867-5
A DOLL'S HOUSE, Henrik Ibsen. 80pp. 27062-9
HEDDA GABLER, Henrik Ibsen. 80pp. 26469-6
THE MISANTHROPE, Molière. 64pp. 27065-3
HAMLET, William Shakespeare. 128pp. 27278-8
JULIUS CAESAR, William Shakespeare. 80pp. 26876-4
MACBETH, William Shakespeare. 96pp. 27802-6
A MIDSUMMER NIGHT'S DREAM, William Shakespeare. 80pp. 27067-X
ROMEO AND JULIET, William Shakespeare. 96pp. 27557-4
ARMS AND THE MAN, George Bernard Shaw. 80pp. (Available in U.S. only.) 26476-9
THE SCHOOL FOR SCANDAL, Richard Brinsley Sheridan. 96pp. 26687-7
ANTIGONE, Sophocles. 64pp. 27804-2
OEDIPUS REX, Sophocles. 64pp. 26877-2
MISS JULIE, August Strindberg. 64pp. 27281-8
THE PLAYBOY OF THE WESTERN WORLD AND RIDERS TO THE SEA, J. M. Synge. 80pp. 27562-0
THE IMPORTANCE OF BEING EARNEST, Oscar Wilde. 64pp. 26478-5

For a complete list of all the Thrift Editions series write for a free
Thrift Editions brochure (58457-7).